ASSERTIVE
COMMUNICATION
Free Yourself

Techniques, Exercises, PNL Techniques, Non-Verbal Communication, Emotional Intelligence and More!

EMMA KELLER

© Copyright 2021 EMMA KELLER

All Rights Reserved

This document is geared towards providing exact and reliable information with regards to the topic and issue covered. The publication is sold with the idea that the publisher is not required to render accounting, officially permitted, or otherwise, qualified services. If advice is necessary, legal or professional, a practiced individual in the profession should be ordered.

From a Declaration of Principles which was accepted and approved equally by a Committee of the American Bar Association and a Committee of Publishers and Associations.

In no way is it legal to reproduce, duplicate, or transmit any part of this document in either electronic means or in printed format. Recording of this publication is strictly prohibited and any storage of this document is not allowed unless with written permission from the publisher. All rights reserved

The information provided herein is stated to be truthful and consistent, in that any liability, in terms of inattention or otherwise, by any usage or abuse of any policies, processes, or directions contained within is the solitary and utter responsibility of the recipient reader. Under no circumstances will any legal responsibility or blame be held against the publisher for any reparation, damages, or monetary loss due to the information herein, either directly or indirectly.

Respective authors own all copyrights not held by the publisher.

The information herein is offered for informational purposes solely, and is universal as so. The presentation of the information is without contract or any type of guarantee assurance.

The trademarks that are used are without any consent, and the publication of the trademark is without permission or backing by the trademark owner. All trademarks and brands within this book are for clarifying purposes only and are the owned by the owners themselves, not affiliated with this document.

CONTENTS

INTRODUCTION 5
    Why be assertive? 7

CHAPTER 1 WHAT IS ASSERTIVE COMMUNICATION? 9
    The three modes of communication 10

CHAPTER 2 THE CHARACTERISTICS OF ASSERTIVENESS 13
    Characteristics of the passive type 15
    Characteristics of the aggressive type 15
    THE CONSTRUCTION OF A COMPETENT ANSWER: THE VERBAL COMPONENTS 16
    THE CONSTRUCTION OF A COMPETENT ANSWER: THE NON-VERBAL COMPONENTS 19
    HOW TO INCREASE OUR NON-VERBAL ASSERTIVE SKILLS 21

CHAPTER 3 ASSERTIVENESS TECHNIQUES 26
    COMMUNICATION TECHNIQUES 27
    THE ASSERTIVE FORMULATION 28
    ASSERTIVE CRITICISM VS MANIPULATIVE CRITICISM 31
    DEFENSE TECHNIQUES 32
    DISARM AGGRESSIVITY 37

CHAPTER 4 EXERCISES TO IMPROVE ASSERTIVENESS 39
    HOW TO LEARN TO BE ASSERTIVE? THE 6 LEVELS: EXCITATORY OR EMOTIONAL EXERCISES 40
    EXERCISES TO BECOME MORE ASSERTIVE 43

CHAPTER 5 EMOTIONAL INTELLIGENCE 45
    Effects and Benefits of Emotional Intelligence on Daily Life 49
    What Emotional Intelligence is NOT 50

CHAPTER 6 EMOTIONAL INTELLIGENCE IN THE COUPLE 52
    5 Emotional intelligence exercises 56

CHAPTER 7 WHAT EMPATHY IS AND HOW TO DEVELOP IT FOR BETTER COMMUNICATION 58

CHAPTER 8 THE RIGHT TO SAY NO 65
    4 SIMPLE TIPS FOR ACTION 69
CHAPTER 9 THE IMPORTANCE OF SETTING BOUNDARIES 70
CHAPTER 10 HOW TO OVERCOME YOUR OWN INSECURITY 75
CHAPTER 11 NON-VERBAL COMMUNICATION 78
    ELEMENTS OF NON-VERBAL COMMUNICATION 80
    CAN BODY LANGUAGE HELP IN INTERPERSONAL RELATIONSHIPS? 84
    HOW TO INTERPRET THE LANGUAGE OF THE BODY 87
    EXAMPLES OF BODY GESTURES AND THEIR USE 89
CHAPTER 12 NLP 95
CHAPTER 13 NLP TECHNIQUES 101
CHAPTER 14 ASSERTIVENESS TECHNIQUES FOR SUCCESS AT WORK 106
CHAPTER 15 HOW TO BE ASSERTIVE IN LIFE AS A COUPLE 111
CONCLUSIONS 121

ASSERTIVE COMMUNICATION

Free Yourself

INTRODUCTION

Assertive communication is a precious tool for finding harmony in the workplace, as well as in interpersonal relationships.

When we communicate with someone, it can happen that misunderstandings are created and that a wrong approach to the other generates tensions, easily avoidable by using the weapon of assertiveness.

But what exactly do we mean by the term assertiveness and why, by becoming assertive, we could improve our relationships with friends, partner, colleagues and the quality of our life?

Assertiveness, from the Latin "asserere", or assert, is the human capacity to express one's emotions and ideas clearly and effectively, without harming the dignity and opinions of others.

Being assertive: where (and how) to start

Assertive communication is the ability to express positive and negative ideas and feelings in an open, honest and direct way. It recognizes and protects our rights while respecting the rights of others.

This is a small assertive communication manual that will guide you in enhancing this skill and developing a respectful approach towards your interlocutors.

We open our guide with a definition of assertiveness, starting from its meaning and the characteristics of this communicative approach.

ASSERTIVE COMMUNICATION

Free Yourself

As we have said, assertiveness is the ability to express and assert one's opinions while respecting the needs and limitations of others. It is not easy to have an assertive attitude: often, even unwittingly, one slips into the sphere of aggression, which does not help relationships between colleagues and risks creating tears in the professional context.

This is why assertiveness and aggression are two absolutely different concepts:

Assertiveness is based on balance. In this case, the balance to be sought is between respecting your opinion and respecting the opinions of others. Assertiveness involves admitting your point of view firmly, fairly and with empathy;

Aggression is based on victory. In this case, the behavior is selfish, based only on the pursuit of personal interests without regard for the rights, needs, feelings or wishes of other people.

In other words, if your boss asks you to do a series of tasks in a few hours the day before you leave for vacation, he is showing aggressive behavior, because he does not take into account your needs and requirements. If, upon the request, you reply that these tasks will be carried out upon your return from vacation, you will assert your rights while respecting the need of your boss, that is to carry out a job.

The three styles of communication

Passive mode: Those who communicate in passive mode usually fear expressing their point of view for fear of being misjudged, making mistakes and not having the approval of others. These people have the role of "victims" and fail to assert their positions because they believe they are not worth enough. Their body communicates closure: the shoulders are bent, the eyes down, the rhythm of the paraverbal communication is slow and wavering.

Aggressive mode: A person with an aggressive approach is characterized by his intransigence in conveying his positions, without any regard for the needs of others. His body language communicates attack and he is prone to raise his voice.

ASSERTIVE COMMUNICATION

Free Yourself

Assertive mode: our goal is to learn how to develop assertive communication, which respects the opinions of others by valuing our needs and their needs.

Why be assertive?

Each of us, based on his experience, can respond to events and situations with a passive, aggressive or assertive way of communicating.

Our goal, however, is to become assertive and to take full advantage of this opportunity by building a positive and trusting climate among other people.

Being assertive as a couple, in the workplace (and beyond) will help you to:

- Develop successful solutions: so-called "win-win" solutions are those that allow both parties to obtain satisfaction from an agreement. An assertive approach favors precisely this type of relationship, facilitating the peaceful resolution of conflicts;
- Be less anxious and stressed;
- Increase your self-esteem and the consideration that others have of you;
- Avoid being exploited or passively subjected to the choices of third parties.

For example, assertive communication offers us the best solution to create a respectful work environment and a climate of trust between colleagues and collaborators. But how do you get to be assertive and take full advantage of this approach?

Say "NO" at the right time: for assertive behavior, you will have to abandon the need to please everyone and do things according to their expectations. If you try to please everyone, in the long run, you will be

ASSERTIVE COMMUNICATION
Free Yourself

dissatisfied and feel weak the next time you try to ask for something you want. Maintain your position and always explain why you won't do it.

Check the tone of your voice: having a tone of voice that is too aggressive could mislead your interlocutor, just as having a tone that is too calm could give him a way to bully you. Be patient and don't get irritated if you end up raising your voice without realizing it or rushing a conversation because you get angry.

Practice "negative assertion": this is a particular assertiveness technique that allows you to look at the negative sides of your behavior with acceptance and positivity without slipping into anxieties or worries. You have to accept your mistakes or flaws, but don't apologize. If you receive negative criticism and are accused, for example, of being distracted, accept it positively and raise with a "Yes, you're right, I don't always listen carefully to what you have to say".

Don't shift the focus of the discussion: the secret to effective communication and better relationship formation is to be aware of exactly what the other person is trying to say. Try not to bring up past problems or find distractions to embarrass your interlocutor.

Pay attention to non-verbal communication: when we talk about non-verbal communication we mean body language, eye contact, posture, listening cues and reactions. Observe all this carefully and try to understand what your interlocutor wants to communicate.

In this guide we will tackle this topic and give you some tips to help you develop this skill and clearly express your wishes without feeling discomfort or guilt. If you're ready, let's get started right away.

ASSERTIVE COMMUNICATION

Free Yourself

CHAPTER 1 WHAT IS ASSERTIVE COMMUNICATION?

When it comes to assertive communication, we inevitably enter into the sphere of interpersonal relationships.

Assertive communication is a healthy premise for the establishment of interpersonal relationships that are not in the name of aggression or passivity. If we are passive, we risk a misrecognition of our needs and soon others will define roles and tasks for us. As a result, we will feel frustrated because we will cease to be ourselves.

If we are aggressive, we bully instead. The coexistence of others with us will inevitably be difficult.

It is important to express our authentic feelings towards the people with whom we enter into a relationship, whatever they are, bearing in mind that there are no negative feelings. The negativity, if anything, lies in denying the feeling.

ASSERTIVE COMMUNICATION AS A BALANCE BETWEEN OPPOSITES

ASSERTIVENESS ARISES AS THE ABILITY TO BALANCE THE TWO COMPONENTS.

Many times we would like to feel free to express our opinions, but just as many times we are afraid of hurting others or of being judged, or we still experience experiences of guilt.

Instead, it is allowed to express ourselves with all the authenticity of our feelings and just as we have the right to implement this, in the same way, the other also has the right to react with his entire range of emotions and feelings. And whether he gets offended or not does not depend on us, but on his sensitivity.

ASSERTIVE COMMUNICATION

Free Yourself

The three modes of communication

It is possible to trace 3 communication styles:

- ✓ Aggressive
- ✓ Passive
- ✓ Assertive

The aggressive person is the one who does not take into account the needs of others, the one who imposes his point of view with prevarication, demands and manipulates. He puts his own desires first, dominates others and uses any means, even destructive ones. These are personalities without empathic abilities and with hostile components.

The passive person is the one who, in order not to upset others, adapts to circumstances, sacrificing their own needs. He does not express moods, represses any dissent and is easily influenced. At the base there is an anxious, repressed and guilty component.

Assertive communication, on the other hand, places us in a position to:

- ✓ Openly and sincerely express opinions, feelings and needs;
- ✓ Respect our rights and those of others equally;
- ✓ Solve problems in a positive and balanced way, considering the points of view of the people involved.

How to communicate assertively?

Aggression.

How do we behave when, for example, our child responds badly to us, a colleague criticizes us in front of everyone, our partner is rude to us?

There are those who keep everything inside, swallowing anger, and there are those who react in a "showy" way by pouring it onto the other and screaming at them, losing their temper in an attempt to "punish" and regain a position of superiority.

ASSERTIVE COMMUNICATION

Free Yourself

Let's take a concrete example: a very dear friend asks us to go and see a film that contrasts with our tastes.

Our reaction could be:

Aggressive: we brutally tell him that the films he sees are really ridiculous or that they don't have enough "depth". Our friend will feel offended, also because, if he is very sensitive, the judgment we have expressed will not be limited by him simply to the film, but also extended to his person! If our reaction was really dry, it is unlikely that this person will make a similar request in the future!

Passive: we are afraid of hurting him and so we satisfy him, perhaps behind there are still a thousand other reasons why we do not want to disappoint him (it is possible that he is going through a negative period, he is alone etc ...). However, complying with his request, we neglect our real interests and the evening spent will seem useless ...

Assertive: we explain motivating our disagreement, in a calm but firm way; we tell him that that film does not reflect the genre we usually watch and we offer an alternative or in any case a way to spend the evening that satisfies both of us. Our friend may be disappointed, but he will understand and we will experience some satisfaction from you being honest with him.

To achieve assertive communication, therefore, it is necessary to implement certain strategies.

It is necessary to comply with some criteria:

Describe the event that occurred, circumscribe it and do not generalize it, always maintaining a sense of proportion; criticism must be constructive. It is good to always criticize the behavior, and never the person. (Not "you are rude", but "when you raised your voice yesterday while we were busy ..."

Highlight the negative impact that that behavior has on us, on a concrete and emotional level. ("... I felt

ASSERTIVE COMMUNICATION
Free Yourself

... and I had to stop ... ")

Explain why it feels the way it does.

Highlight the desired change and the positive consequences.

Emphasize the persistence of negative consequences in the event that the change does not take place.

Express the will to solve the problem in a collaborative perspective.

The moment we reveal information about ourselves and our real feelings to others, we get naked, the relationship becomes deeper and more sincere, and we are more likely to be understood.

Assertiveness and self-esteem: two elements that are intertwined

Assertiveness and self-esteem are mutually linked, so self-confidence determines a greater perception of control and influence on external events and on how to solve problems: if we manage to act assertive, the esteem we have of ourselves changes in a positive sense and, consequently, it too benefits.

ASSERTIVE COMMUNICATION
Free Yourself

CHAPTER 2 THE CHARACTERISTICS OF ASSERTIVENESS

We could define assertiveness as that point of balance between a passive and an aggressive communication style.

With it, a communicative style is adopted that allows the individual to express their opinions, their emotions and to commit themselves to positively solving situations and problems. There is no absolutely definable assertive response, it must be evaluated within the social situation and is a continuous process of adjusting one's communicative performance.

Assertive behavior is therefore not intermediate between aggressive and passive behavior: the goal for assertive communication is the ability to reduce one's aggressive and passive components. Assertiveness is a way of communicating that comes from the harmony between social skills, emotions and rationality without necessarily changing one's personality.

In this integration the neurovegetative aspect comes into play for emotions, the voluntary motor for gestures and actions and finally the cortical-cognitive one for thoughts and verbalizations. Between these three aspects of the personality there is a relationship of interdependence whereby improving assertiveness means acting on each of the three. Not only is it important to know the techniques to improve assertiveness, but it is necessary to develop new behavioral habits and perfect the education of feelings and emotions. Getting familiar with the world of feelings requires, in fact, "a sentimental education".

ASSERTIVE COMMUNICATION

Free Yourself

The conceptual structure of assertiveness is the order that everyone places in his life, when he thinks about himself and interacts with other people with greater awareness.

This way of acting makes it possible to establish an active and intelligent relationship which is based on the correct assessment of the situation and on having the adequate means available to be able to choose the most appropriate solution. The construct of assertiveness is constituted by the idea of freedom as the ability to free oneself from negative environmental conditionings and includes the knowledge of oneself and one's personality, of the theory of assertive rights (this includes the idea of reciprocity, i.e. the same right to communicate desires and beliefs and to pursue individual goals is also recognized to others, the ability to recognize and criticize the irrational ideas that generate and maintain emotional discomfort and disturbances).

The second aspect concerns the form of assertiveness, that is the ability to express oneself in a more evolved and effective way, thus translated into non-verbal and verbal skills, and, more generally, into social competence. This aspect has been defined by L. Philips (1968) as "the extent to which the individual is able to communicate with others, in order to satisfy rights, needs, motivations and obligations, to a reasonable extent and without prejudice to similar rights of other people, in the form of free and open dialogue". In this case, the assertive person knows how to express emotions, feelings, needs and personal beliefs in a clear and technically effective way, increasingly reducing feelings of anxiety, discomfort or aggression.

CHARACTERISTICS OF THE ASSERTIVE PERSON

Assertiveness is an effective behavior technique if it is an integral part of our attitude.

Those with an assertive style are recognizable by some physical signals of verbal and non-verbal communication.

The same goes for people who tend to be passive or aggressive. Any self-diagnosis shows that it is difficult for a person to be just passive or aggressive or assertive. In each one different degree of these tendential behaviors coexist. It is important to be aware of what prevails over others.

We need to be assertive about ourselves:

1) Peacefully recognize your limits
2) Set realistic goals for change
3) Avoid being blackmailed

This communication modality is contrasted by a passive and aggressive communication style.

Characteristics of the passive type

The subject with a passive communication style thinks more about pleasing others than himself, is easily influenced and undergoes situations without opposing. He is a person who has high social anxiety, who is unable to adequately express their needs and requirements. His goal is to obtain the consent of all and to avoid any form of conflict with others. In the short term, this type of attitude is useful for reducing anxiety, but it ends up significantly limiting the person's ability to act. At the base of this attitude there are often feelings of guilt associated with a strong anxiety component.

Characteristics of the aggressive type

The subject with this style is a person who does not respect the limits of others, is focused on his own desires without paying attention to those around him. To do this, he uses any means at his disposal, even

ASSERTIVE COMMUNICATION

Free Yourself

destructive and violent. The tendency is to dominate others and the only goal that is set is personal and social power. At the base of this type of behavior there are still some components of anxiety accompanied by anger and hostility. There is also contempt for others and a failure to recognize the dignity of others.

The conceptual structure of assertiveness is based on the functionality of five levels, each of which defines an aspect.

Verbal characteristics in social interactions

Communicative behaviors are emitted mainly through two independents but subtly linked channels: the non-verbal channel and the verbal channel. There is a simple distinction to understand and discriminate the aspects and the complexity of the relationship between verbal and non-verbal: what is said is not only important, but how it is said is fundamental; not only the what, but also the how, therefore.

It goes without saying that to obtain a valid interaction, the non-verbal communication must be congruent with the verbal one. Social research indicates that the effect on communication of non-verbal aspects is four times greater than verbal characteristics.

THE CONSTRUCTION OF A COMPETENT ANSWER: THE VERBAL COMPONENTS

They are skills that allow us to communicate with others in a way that is adequate and in keeping with our needs and also allow us to defend ourselves without suffering, without generating in us adaptations or excessive reactions to manipulation or criticism.

They are those that allow us to start, maintain and end a conversation, to know how to ask questions, to give generic or personal information according to the needs of verbal interrelation.

ASSERTIVE COMMUNICATION

Free Yourself

CLOSED QUESTIONS

These provide a short answer (yes / no) and are intended to end the conversation early. They can be useful at the beginning of a speech.

OPEN QUESTIONS (What, Where, When, Why, How, With whom?)

Open questions, on the other hand, are structured in such a way as to obtain a greater amount of information. Knowing how to ask questions is a priority assertive skill, to create relationships, verify ideas, ask for news, demonstrate and arouse interest.

GIVE AND RECEIVE FREE INFORMATION

This is information that exceeds demand or is given without being solicited (especially concerning one's own interests). Grasping the clues provided by the interlocutor, what is important and interesting for him and paying attention to him allows not to make the conversation an interview and communication can proceed more fluidly.

SELF-OPENING

Communicate the way of thinking, of living, in a non-invasive way, giving information about one's life, one's interests, without monopolizing communication or with the desire to "show off". It is another skill to make communication more dynamic and engaging.

PROTECTIVE SKILLS

Faced with a criticism that can be manipulative, aggressive, non-constructive, there can be various ways of reacting. Discomfort can be addressed by adopting flight behaviors, passive adaptations or attack reactions: these behaviors are not valid. It is necessary to use techniques that allow you to maintain control of the situation.

PERSISTENCE OR BROKEN DISK

This consists of repeating one's point of view with extreme calm, always using the same words, without getting involved in the manipulative strategies of the other, remaining focused on the objective of the interaction. Likewise, it is useful to use this technique when making a

ASSERTIVE COMMUNICATION

Free Yourself

request that it is our right to demand. In order not to fall into a logical-manipulative trap, it is advisable not to ask open questions (eg: why ..?) Or answer the whys of others, with excuses, justifications or explanations. What matters is the systematic repetition of what we want and don't want.

ANIMALIZATION

This consists of accepting criticism by admitting that there may be some truth, without justifying oneself: "I understand your point of view", "You are probably right", or paraphrase, reformulating in the interaction; the answer to the request is to "confuse", accepting the criticism leveled at us and admitting that there may be some truth in it. The goal is to calm down those who criticize us, "displacing them", and then open a clarifying dialogue. You listen to what the person says and using the other person's words or the like, you recognize his need but you declare your point of view.

NEGATIVE ASSERTION

With this formula we admit our mistake and apologize, without feeling anxiety or diminishing our personal image. Negative assertion reduces hostility and tends to extinguish manipulation. Recognizing one's mistake, without however feeling the annoying aftermath of guilt, admitting it in all serenity, is liberating but also natural because the image we give of ourselves is a non-rigid image, not to be questioned by a mistake. This technique dismantles the opponent and takes away animosity towards us.

NEGATIVE INQUIRY

This consists of asking about criticism. If it is a manipulative criticism, we will be able more easily to narrow the scope, focusing it on specific behaviors. Eg: "Were you not interested in the meeting this morning? Why? What didn't you like? Which part would you have liked to be deepened? " Or "Could you please tell me where I went wrong?"

SELECTIVE DISCRIMINATION

ASSERTIVE COMMUNICATION

Free Yourself

This consists of grasping, in a negative, critical message, only that part which we are willing to discuss, to give justifications, to give explanations. It is a question of grasping only that part of the question on which we have data, which can be answered.

DISARMING AGGRESSIVITY

This consists of opposing a criticism that has particularly violent connotations, with extremely calm behavior, conditioning our participation in communication to a decrease in the aggressiveness of the other. Learning these verbal protective skills requires gradual daily training, trying and trying again, simulating the various situations from time to time.

THE CONSTRUCTION OF A COMPETENT ANSWER: THE NON-VERBAL COMPONENTS

Any person, when communicating, whether consciously or unconsciously, uses techniques that are characteristic of his behavioral style (dominance, submission ...) and that favor the passage, the outward and return journey, of the interaction.

The individual through the posture of the body, the expression and the way of gesturing, the intonation and the volume of the voice, establishes relationships with others, at different levels, depending on how they manifest themselves.

Even the non-assertive person uses non-verbal communication techniques, which are however a source of anxiety as they do not facilitate the flow and growth of the interaction or even alter it.

The gestural, facial, bodily, postural expressiveness of our body, but also the way we dress, our look, are part of non-verbal communication, it is our body language.

ASSERTIVE COMMUNICATION

Free Yourself

Non-verbal characteristics in social interactions are:

- Eye contact
- Facial expression
- Gestures
- Body attitude (posture)
- Management of interpersonal space
- Tone, volume and rhythm of the voice
- Physical contact

Eye contact

The person who is able to maintain good eye contact shows himself to be open and confident in what he is saying. Looking directly at another person when you are speaking is an effective way of declaring that you are sincere about what you are saying, and that it is directed at them.

FACIAL EXPRESSION

Have you ever seen someone try to express anger while smiling or laughing? It's just not possible! Effective affirmations require an expression that matches the message. Through facial expressions, the emotions we are experiencing are transmitted in a rather unequivocal way. An assertive person has a good and congruous facial expression that accompanies what they are saying.

MANAGEMENT

The movements of the hands and other parts of the body to describe, emphasize or accompany the speech, should be like nods of the head, arms open and not folded, hands that do not exceed the height of the elbows, and shoulders straight. A message accentuated by appropriate gestures has more emphasis (excessive gesticulation can be distracting!).

POSTURE

ASSERTIVE COMMUNICATION

Free Yourself

When we are comfortable, we feel relaxed and our body reflects this state; an upright, relaxed, open, non-rigid, tense, slumped or bent posture is a telltale sign. The "weight" of your messages to others will be increased if you stand in front of your interlocutor, standing close enough, keeping your head erect.

SPACE MANAGEMENT

Establishing and maintaining a correct interpersonal distance, neither too near, nor too distant, is a distinctive feature of the assertive person; in our culture the optimal distance is one meter, less in the case of intimate or confidential relationships.

TONE AND VOLUME OF THE VOICE

In this way we can communicate our mood, our intentions, our emotions; a clear, relaxed, friendly, well-balanced, non-strained voice is characteristic of the assertive person. A monotonous whisper will rarely convince another person that you are talking about something important, while a shouted epithet will provoke his communication defenses. A medium and well-modulated way of speaking is convincing without intimidating.

PHYSICAL CONTACT

To establish and maintain a sense of intimacy and solidarity, it can generate anxiety in certain situations or with some people; assertive ability is the discrimination of interaction and timing of the use of physical contact.

HOW TO INCREASE OUR NON-VERBAL ASSERTIVE SKILLS

Learn to discriminate the styles of behavior of others by observing the non-verbal characteristics of communication (emotions, role, social status).

ASSERTIVE COMMUNICATION

Free Yourself

Identify the areas in our non-verbal behavior in which we are deficient and train ourselves (from neutral situations to the least anxious to the most anxious).

The assertive levels

The conceptual structure of assertiveness is based on the functionality of five levels, each of which defines an aspect. The first level is constituted by the ability to recognize emotions, the objective of which is emotional autonomy and the perception of emotions without the negative involvement linked to the presence of other people (blushing, stammering, being ashamed, etc.).

The second level: the ability to communicate emotions and feelings, even negative ones, through multiple communication tools represents the second level concerning freedom of expression, i.e. the control of motor reactions without these being altered or inhibited by anxiety and tension.

At the third level we find the awareness of one's rights in the sense of having respect for oneself and for others. It plays a central role in assertiveness theory as the distinction between aggressive, passive and assertive behaviors is based on rights and the principle of reciprocity.

The fourth level is the willingness to appreciate oneself and others.

This implies self-esteem, the ability to enhance the positive aspects of the experience with a functional and constructive vision of one's social role.

The last level is related to the ability to self-fulfill and to be able to decide the aims of one's life. To achieve this, it is necessary to have positive self-image, confidence and personal security.

Having these characteristics involves a greater capacity for self-control, intervention in situations and problem solving, a relaxing "internal environment" that allows difficulties to be perceived not as negative opportunities for frustration, but as obstacles to be skilfully overcome.

ASSERTIVE COMMUNICATION

Free Yourself

The objectives of the various levels are achieved by intervening both on the conceptual aspect, of content, and on the technical aspect, concerning ways of acting and communicating.

Assertive rights

Assertive rights include respect for oneself, one's needs, feelings and beliefs. These rights are necessary to build positive feelings and thoughts such as self-esteem and trust. Recognizing and respecting them also means recognizing and respecting them in others.

Being assertive is not easy, it costs sacrifice and constant exercise in order to obtain satisfactory results. It is important, however, to start practicing, even one concept at a time. As you manage to overcome one, move on to the next. As a Zen aphorism says, "a journey is made up of a thousand steps". We begin, one step at a time, to make the journey towards assertiveness.

In summary, it can be said that assertiveness, bearing in mind one's goals and interests, is the most immediate and direct manifestation of emotions, feelings, needs and personal beliefs, but balancing, depending on the circumstances, aggression and passivity, in order to obtain the best advantage or the least disadvantage for themselves, both in the short and long term.

The right to act in order to guarantee one's dignity. Your own happiness, and satisfaction, to achieve your goals and plans without violating the rights of others.

The right to have and express feelings and emotions.

The right to ask for help.

The right to ask for information.

ASSERTIVE COMMUNICATION

Free Yourself

The right to say no without feeling guilty.

The right to say I don't know.

The right to be wrong.

The right to change your mind.

The right to take your time before giving an answer.

The right to do less than what is the limit of what is humanly possible.

The right to feel good about ourselves regardless of the conditions or opinions of others, without feeling guilty.

And again, the right ....

To do anything, as long as it doesn't harm anyone else.

To maintain your dignity by acting assertively, even if it hurts someone else, provided the motive is assertive and not aggressive.

To make requests to another person, since I recognize the same right of the other person to refuse.

To discuss the problem with the person concerned, and to come to a clarification.

To implement your rights and to respect others' rights.

To have ideas, opinions, personal points of view that do not necessarily coincide with those of others.

That your ideas, opinions and points of view are at least listened to and taken into consideration (not necessarily shared) by other people.

To have needs different from those of other people.

To try certain moods and to manifest them in an assertive way if you decide to do so.

To make mistakes, in good faith.

To decide to raise a certain issue or, conversely, not to raise it.

ASSERTIVE COMMUNICATION
Free Yourself

To really be oneself, even if this sometimes means contravening external expectations.

To be treated with respect and dignity.

To be heard and taken seriously.

To assess your own needs, to prioritize and make personal decisions.

To ask for what is considered more just and opportune, respecting the reciprocal right to refuse the interlocutor.

To change.

To get what you paid for.

To be independent.

To decide what to do with things of your own exclusive relevance (body, time), without infringing the rights of others.

To achieve your goals and to be successful.

To feel pleasure.

To rest and relax.

To engage in activities that are considered useful, stimulating and functional to your well-being.

To give your life a personal imprint.

To love and be loved according to one's true inclination.

Not to suffer emotional blackmail.

To choose ways and times to express your feelings of affection and fidelity.

To develop one's own personal belief in transcendental and immanent values.

ASSERTIVE COMMUNICATION

Free Yourself

CHAPTER 3 ASSERTIVENESS TECHNIQUES

Assertive techniques are communication skills that focus on the content.

That is what to say, with which words to build the message we want to communicate. This does not mean that non-verbal communication is not important in assertiveness.

Indeed, it is taken for granted that in assertive communication to use these techniques you must remain calm but resolute.

In fact, an aggressive attitude can provoke aggression or hostility in the interlocutor, while a passive attitude will make it difficult to assert one's point of view.

We will see here the main assertiveness techniques. The attentive reader must consider them tools and not magic formulas. This means that to be assertive they must be integrated with other skills and, above all, with a certain practice.

These techniques are like a craftsman's tools. Having a toolbox at home is not enough to be able to be an electrician.

The greatest effectiveness of these techniques is in the management of criticism and aggression of others, so as to assert one's point of view and, above all, to be respected and not to be bullied by others.

Assertive techniques fall into two categories:

Communication techniques

These allow you to develop better communication skills. How to start, maintain and end a conversation. But also, to direct it where we prefer.

ASSERTIVE COMMUNICATION

Free Yourself

<u>Defense techniques</u>

These techniques allow you to manage criticism, aggression or manipulative behavior. More simply, they can allow us to manage an insistent salesman or a boss who criticizes us in a surly and incomprehensible way.

COMMUNICATION TECHNIQUES

Assertive communication techniques overlap with the topics covered in effective communication.

Closed or open questions

If you know how to ask the right questions, you can influence the other person's response and the direction of the conversation. I come from years of clinics where you learn to pay close attention to questions, which are often underestimated.

A closed question can only be answered 'yes / no'.

They are used to get precise information but block the normal scrolling of conversations. These are questions like: 'Have you been to the meeting?'

You know those boring people who bombard you with closed questions as if it were an interview? Here it becomes annoying.

Open questions, on the other hand, leave you room for different and articulated answers. Such as 'what do you usually like to eat?', 'What do you do?', 'What topics were discussed in the meeting?' Open-ended questions are useful for fostering conversation and extracting more information from the other. They usually start with who, how, what, when, where or why.

Because usually, however, it risks being perceived as aggressive and judgmental. It would be better to use 'How come?'

ASSERTIVE COMMUNICATION

Free Yourself

Free information

Free information is information that we give without being asked for. A person says something simply because they feel like it, or to add something to the conversation.

This provides opportunities to continue the conversation and make it more authentic. Try to observe people you find nice, good communicators, or with whom you can easily talk, and observe when they resort to free information.

Self-opening

Self-openings are all unsolicited personal information that we tell the interlocutor. It is a very effective technique to put others at ease but also to create bonds with people and, depending on the contexts in which it is used, also to gain credibility.

Those who speak in public and share some anecdotes from their personal history manage to capture the attention of the public. You can begin to foster authentic relationships between colleagues.

Much of the success of slimming products and programs was based on testimonials, before and after photos and their self-openings that led the future customer to identify with them and their problems, now overcome.

THE ASSERTIVE FORMULATION

Practice the following tips if you want to develop assertive language. Please pay special attention to the first point. That is to use the first person singular. This trick may seem simple but it allows you to manage difficult conversations without causing negative reactions from the other person.

ASSERTIVE COMMUNICATION
Free Yourself

Think of the difference in hearing you say, 'When you do this you really piss me off!' compared to 'I get really mad when ...' If you accuse me of making you angry, I will tell you that I do not make you angry, and we end up arguing about this.

If you tell me you're getting mad, who am I to tell you it's not true?

Use first-person affirmations, be clear and direct:

'I would like you to refund me'.

'I think what you did is good, but I'd like you to ...'

Use verbs like 'I think', 'I believe', 'I want', 'I would like', 'I expect'. In this way you express yourself and do not refer to universal rules or blame or manipulate the other.

Stick to the facts and don't generalize. 'You are late for the fourth time this week' and not 'you are always late' which is an unrealistic accusation and provokes hostility in the other who starts arguing about the falsity of the claim.

Describe how the other person's behavior makes you feel, this makes people aware of the consequences of their actions:

'When you raise your voice, you scare me ... I'd rather you speak more quietly'.

'When you don't tell me how you feel about it you make me confused'.

Hold your position - use the broken record technique. This involves thinking about what you want, preparing something to say and then repeating it as long as necessary:

'I would like you to refund me... Yes, but I would still like a refund... I understand what you are saying but I still want a refund'.

ASSERTIVE COMMUNICATION

Free Yourself

CRITICIZE IN A CONSTRUCTIVE WAY

Some people think constructive criticism doesn't exist. It is not easy to know how to constructively criticize, but it is a necessary skill in the world of work and often in private life as well.

The encyclopedia defines criticism thus:

Intellectual faculty that enables men to examine and evaluate their work and the result or results of their activity in order to choose, select, distinguish the true from the false, the certain from the probable, the beautiful from the less beautiful or the ugly, the good from the bad or less good, etc.

In order to speak of assertive criticism, we must immediately correct something: first of all, the evaluation of people. The criticism is always of the behavior and never of the person.

Then one must also get rid of rigid and general judgments such as right / wrong. You only state your point of view - in the first person.

What we mean by constructive criticism is an assertive statement. The aim is to make the interlocutor aware of what we think and how his specific behavior makes us feel and not him as a person.

Others never know what we expect from them. So, if we want a change in someone's behavior, we have to say it explicitly.

Constructive criticism:

It is directed at the specific behavior: 'you are late today, and it is the fourth time this week' and not 'you are always late'.

It is formulated assertively in the first person without accusations: 'this bothers me a lot and I have no intention of ignoring violations of working hours' and, 'it disrespects me and the company'.

State what behavior is expected of the other: 'I expect you to be here no later than nine in the morning and the days to follow' and 'you must stop being late'.

ASSERTIVE COMMUNICATION
Free Yourself

If you want, it can be concluded with an appreciation of the person and a demonstration of confidence in his abilities: 'I know that you are a valid member of our team and I want to have you with us'.

ASSERTIVE CRITICISM VS MANIPULATIVE CRITICISM

MANIPULATIVE CRITICISM

Is aimed at the person,

Is imprecise or generalizes,

Aims to blame the other,

Tends to close the dialogue,

Generates anger, anxiety and guilt,

Is not about behavior.

Constructive criticism

Is accurate,

Aims to improve performance,

Keeps the dialogue open,

Does not offend the other person.

OTHER TIPS FOR BETTER MANAGING CRITICISM TOWARDS OTHERS:

1. Contact the person concerned rather than an intermediary.
2. Speak privately rather than publicly.

ASSERTIVE COMMUNICATION

Free Yourself

3. Avoid comparisons.
4. Protest verbally and not with facial expressions.
5. Avoid humor and irony.
6. Don't let a problem pile up, the sooner you tackle it the better.
7. Tackle one topic at a time.
8. Don't apologize.
9. Don't use words like 'never', 'always' or 'you must'.
10. Try to be concrete and precise.
11. Refer to the other's value system.
12. Talk about yourself instead of the interlocutor, using the first person singular.
13. Present the positive aspect of criticism.
14. Suggest a realistic and acceptable solution.

Remember that when you are talking with another person you are presenting two different ways of feeling and thinking, influenced by different experiences and expectations. Two different points of view and no objective reality.

DEFENSE TECHNIQUES

Defense techniques help you to defend yourself from the aggression of others. The best-known defense techniques are:

Negative assertion - to accept constructive or assertive criticism.

Negative inquiry - to handle manipulative or aggressive criticism.

The broken record - to hold your own position and avoid arguments.

Glamor - to manage aggressive or manipulative behaviors.

Disarming aggression - to manage aggressive or manipulative behaviors.

Selectively ignore - to manage aggressive or manipulative behavior.

ASSERTIVE COMMUNICATION
Free Yourself

NEGATIVE ASSERTION: HOW TO ACCEPT CRITICISM

A good way to deal with a criticism motivated by our mistake is to accept and admit your faults. Openly state that what you did was unintentional and make yourself available to make up for it.

This technique is called negative assertion and if used well, it eliminates both the aggression of others and one's own anxiety and embarrassment.

Negative assertion involves apologizing, acknowledging your faults, explaining that they were not intentional, and proposing to remedy them.

Example

We are in the office with a colleague who criticizes us for a delay on some deliveries.

'Yes sorry, the delay was my fault. It wasn't my intention, I thought I could finish all the orders on time. '

Apologize: 'excuse me'.

Admitting guilt: 'my fault'.

Declare unintentionality: 'it was not my intention'.

If possible, try to fix it: 'can I do something to fix it?'

Avoid trivializing in order not to take responsibility.

NEGATIVE INQUIRY

Negative inquiry is used to deal with different types of criticism. It consists in asking about criticism. If constructive criticism lies behind the criticism, we gain important information about our behavior. If, on the other hand, it is only aggression or an attempt at manipulation, the interlocutor will no longer know what to answer and will interrupt the

ASSERTIVE COMMUNICATION

Free Yourself

conversation in frustration. The aim is to bring the other person to be concrete and specific in the criticism of us.

We will begin by conditionally admitting the error and continue the communication by asking questions about the opinion of the critic.

Example

Criticism: 'Your work is far from perfect'.

Answer: 'What exactly do you mean?'

Criticism: 'If you write like this nobody will understand you'.

Answer: 'Is there anything else that makes my work imperfect?'

Criticism: 'It seems to me that you don't care about your job'.

Answer: 'Why does this bother you?'

Criticism: 'Because then I have to remedy your mistakes'.

Answer: 'Ah, ok! The next time you feel compelled to correct my mistakes, I'd like you to let me know so we can understand each other better.'

Types of questions you can ask:

Ask for an explanation of what the interlocutor means.

Ask what he would have done in your place.

Ask what mistakes have been made.

Ask what they recommend you do.

BROKEN DISK

This technique consists of repeating over and over, just like a broken record returning to the same position, your point of view. The difficult

ASSERTIVE COMMUNICATION
Free Yourself

thing is to do it calmly, without being trapped in the discussions, questions or provocations of the interlocutor.

In conversation, nothing else needs to be said other than the sentence that expresses our intentions.

Example

A: 'Can you stay to finish this presentation tonight?'

B: 'I'm sorry, but I can't today'.

A: 'It's important, and you're the only one who can do it.'

B: 'I'm really sorry. But today I can't stay.'

A: 'Usually you are always available, I was counting on you'.

B: 'I'm sorry I can't help you, but I have to leave at six today.'

Don't use excuses like 'I already have other commitments'. If you want to use excuses, that's fine, but you need to be aware that it's passive and non-assertive behavior. The aim is not to get involved in the conversation, not to come up with an apology.

GLAMOR

The fog technique is the easiest to use. At first glance it may seem that it goes against some principles of assertiveness. In fact, it consists in continuing to remain vague by replying continuously 'maybe', and 'it may be'.

In short, avoiding open communication. In this case the purpose is precisely to 'cloud' the interlocutor. Where the limits of a direct and open approach are recognized, we resort to disorienting.

ASSERTIVE COMMUNICATION

Free Yourself

This is for very practical reasons. In some situations, in fact, it may be useless or even counterproductive to clarify one's thoughts. In short, the lesser of evils is chosen. This technique is often integrated with others.

In many discussions with aggressive tones, the answers are given starting from what we say. If we say nothing, we give nothing that the other can cling to attack us.

You can also openly deny that you want to address the topic: 'This is not the right time to talk about these topics', 'It embarrasses me to talk about these things', 'These are not topics that I like to talk about'. But also, to start changing the subject by talking about something else: 'What a beautiful day', 'In Italy you don't work anymore', etc. It is useful when you are confronted with people who are not willing to dialogue. This technique is intended as a premise for future clarification.

Example

A: 'You always want to be right about everything, you can't talk'.

B: 'It may be (glamor), but why does he say this? (Negative investigation)'.

A: 'Where would we be if we all did this?'

B: 'Forget it.'

A: 'She wasn't correct!'

B: 'It's possible'.

A: 'His way of working is wrong.'

B: 'There are those who are better, but there is no need to insist'.

A: 'If I did that, they would fire me'.

B: 'Maybe, in Italy we work badly'.

A: 'Oh that's for sure'.

B: 'At least we have the technology that helps us'.

ASSERTIVE COMMUNICATION

Free Yourself

DISARM AGGRESSIVITY

This technique is used to respond to a person who criticizes violently. The goal is to 'disarm' aggression. That is to avoid anger taking over and turning into violence, calming the interlocutor.

To disarm others' aggression, you need to adopt a calm attitude. In the meantime, leave aside the topic of discussion while inviting the interlocutor to calm down.

For example, you might talk about politics and see the other get aggressive. As long as you are discussing politics, your interlocutor will continue to get angry. Also, if you start to have an aggressive tone, even unknowingly, you will make things even worse.

For this reason, letting go of the subject of politics and concentrating on staying calm removes two elements that cause others to be aggressive. You can then ask the other to calm down but be careful: if done in a clumsy way you will get the opposite result. It is essential to speak calmly. Telling a person to calm down aggressively only makes things worse.

Example

A: 'I understand that talking about this subject bothers you. After you've calmed down, we'll talk about anything you want'.

If the person does not accept it, it is best to stop the discussion. It may be best to leave the person alone until they calm down. Taking care to make yourself available to return to the topic later.

SELECTIVELY IGNORE

This technique consists of responding only to those parts of the criticism that are accepted. Ignoring those that are considered manipulative. You

ASSERTIVE COMMUNICATION
Free Yourself

have to try to ignore some parts of the criticism, and answer only the sensible ones.

This allows you to let the aggression run out by shifting the attention to a constructive part of the criticism.

Example

A: 'I have been waiting for your technician for three weeks and you keep telling me that he will arrive the next day. I'm tired of dealing with the clueless! You sell me hardware that breaks and then you don't even come to fix it. If you don't solve the problem today, we will change suppliers!'

B: 'If I understand correctly, you asked for our intervention starting three weeks ago. I am sorry that the problem has not been solved. Do you remember who you spoke to and the exact date of the first report?'

HOW LEARNING WORKS

I can never say it enough. Changing your behavior and emotional reactions is not easy. It is more like learning a sport than geography. If I tell you that the capital of Texas is Austin, you have learned that. If I describe you as a top serve in tennis, it is not my fault if you are not able to do it.

You have to understand the theory, but above all you have to do a lot of practice. You have to learn to feel the racket and the feedback it gives to the hand. You have to automate the movements.

If you approach these techniques like geography, you'll waste time and you will not go anywhere.

ASSERTIVE COMMUNICATION
Free Yourself

CHAPTER 4 EXERCISES TO IMPROVE ASSERTIVENESS

If you want to test your assertiveness level more thoroughly, you can answer these questions:

Can you express your negative emotions to others without using offensive phrases or words?

Are you able to show and express your strengths?

Can you recognize the successes of others and compliment them?

Do you have the ability to confidently claim what you are entitled to?

Can you accept criticism without getting defensive?

Do you feel comfortable when you receive a compliment?

Are you able to assert your rights?

Do you have the ability to refuse unreasonable requests from friends, family or colleagues?

Can you easily strike up and carry on a conversation?

Do you ask for help when you need it?

Affirmative answers indicate an assertive approach. The more affirmative the answers are, the closer your behavior is to assertive style.

ASSERTIVE COMMUNICATION

Free Yourself

BARRIERS TO ASSERTIVITY

If the assertive style is the most effective for communicating one's needs, why is it so difficult to put it into practice? The answer is in the following statement:

"Assertiveness isn't in what you do, it's about who you are."

Therefore, there may be some aspects of our personality that prevent us from being assertive. Let's look at some of these barriers:

Lack of confidence in communicating opinions or needs to others.

Likewise, overconfidence could be a hindrance in the same way.

Being overly focused on satisfying one's own needs, refusing to take those of others into consideration.

Poor listening skills.

Be focused on pleasing others and assessing their needs as most important.

Constant worry of being judged by others.

HOW TO LEARN TO BE ASSERTIVE? THE 6 LEVELS: EXCITATORY OR EMOTIONAL EXERCISES

Obstacles and barriers can be overcome. It is possible to learn to be assertive. To do this, it is important to believe in yourself and mentally set yourself up for change.

There are a number of assertive communication techniques, which can prove useful if applied consistently. Andrew Salter (1961), the behavioral psychologist and hypnotherapist, founder of Assertiveness

ASSERTIVE COMMUNICATION

Free Yourself

Training, summarizes them in what he calls the "6 Excitatory or Emotional Exercises" which we can summarize as follows:

Use words that describe your emotions: "I enjoy it when ..."; "I feel uncomfortable when ...".

Use the non-verbal component - use facial expressions when communicating.

Practice communicating your views to express disagreement when necessary.

Practice using the "I": "I wish that ..."; "I need ..."; "I feel ..."

Practice accepting compliments without undermining them.

Improvise and act spontaneously.

Here are some useful tips for taking the assertiveness path:

1. Recognize your wants and needs

If we become aware of our needs and desires, we will be able to understand when they are not being met, giving us the opportunity to do something. We all have basic needs. Knowing them allows us to communicate them. Pay attention to what is important to you.

2. Accept criticism

Criticism, when constructive, can open the door to growth and awareness. Being assertive does not mean being perfect and immune to criticism. On the contrary, it involves knowing how to question yourself when necessary. If no one gives you criticism or remarks, ask for some. It is a chance for improvement.

3. Respect the needs of others

Being assertive means communicating your needs firmly and respectfully, but it is equally important to listen to the needs of other

ASSERTIVE COMMUNICATION

Free Yourself

people. For this, it is necessary to actively listen to others, trying to understand their point of view.

4. Follow the basic rules of assertive communication

There are some simple communication rules that might be helpful to follow:

Use the "I". It helps to convey one's needs in a direct and clear way.

Say "No." Helps define boundaries.

Be clear. Going around things doesn't help communicate your needs in a way that is understood.

Trust. Don't delay too much, avoid postponing your decisions.

Stay calm. Remember, becoming aggressive often means losing control!

5. Be aware that you cannot control the reactions of others. Use the acronym LADDER to remember

Don't take responsibility for the reaction's others may have to your assertive behavior. If they acted aggressively or resentfully, avoid reacting in the same way.

Remember that you can only control yourself and your reactions, so do your best to stay calm and measure your behavior.

To the extent that you show respect for the needs of others, you have the right to express your wishes and rights. LADDER is an acronym that guides you, step by step, to the use of assertive communication. This strategy works best when you want to talk to someone about a certain topic.

Here's how it works:

L stands for LOOK - Become aware of your needs and rights; try to understand what you feel in that situation.

ASSERTIVE COMMUNICATION

Free Yourself

A stands for ARRANGE - Arrange a discussion with the other person to discuss the situation.

D stands for DEFINE - Define the problem specifically. For example "I know you love Thai food, but we went to eat it the last two times. I'd like to try a different place."

D stands for DESCRIBE - Describe your feelings so that the other person understands how you feel. For example "I'm sorry when you don't consider my point of view".

E stands for EXPRESS - Express what you want clearly and concisely. For example "Today I'd like to eat pizza".

R stands for REINFORCE - Reinforce the other person by explaining the mutual benefits of taking the option you suggested. For example "We both like pizza and we can meet our old friends by going to a pizzeria".

EXERCISES TO BECOME MORE ASSERTIVE

Here are some simple exercises to practice and build your assertive skills.

1. **Role Play**

To be assertive it is important to understand your own and others' needs. To practice this skill, the best strategy is to use role play. A useful technique is the one called "perspective activity". Arrange two chairs facing each other. As you sit in the left-hand chair, imagine communicating your needs. When you think you have communicated them adequately, take the perspective of the other person being considered and communicate on that basis. Keep moving from chair to chair by practicing flexibly adopting both perspectives.

2. **Construction of sentences**

ASSERTIVE COMMUNICATION

Free Yourself

Think of any situation. Now try to develop sentences of an assertive nature and work to communicate your message to the fullest.

Example: Taking into consideration the situation presented at the beginning of the chapter, here are some useful examples:

"If you need anything, just let me know, I'll gladly help you."

"Can you ask me next time you need something from my bag please? Thanks."

Now, think of any scenario in your mind and come up with 2 or 3 assertive sentences imagining that you are communicating what you want.

3. Practice using non-verbal communication

We talked about assertiveness in terms of verbal communication. But it is equally important to consider non-verbal communication. Research shows that assertive people are able to maintain eye contact and good body posture. Therefore:

Maintain eye contact during communication. You will convey confidence in what you say.

Lean forward slightly as you listen to someone's opinion. You will give the impression that you are listening attentively to their opinion.

Nod your head. You will convey you are listening actively.

Avoid aggressive facial expressions. You will give the impression of being able to remain calm and confident in yourself.

Pay attention to the tone of voice used. Make sure you are polite and respectful of others' point of view.

Don't think you have to change overnight! Take your time and take it one step at a time. Assertiveness will become part of you without too much effort.

ASSERTIVE COMMUNICATION
Free Yourself

CHAPTER 5 EMOTIONAL INTELLIGENCE

Emotional intelligence is defined as the ability of an individual to recognize, distinguish, label and manage their own and others' emotions.

The concept of emotional intelligence is relatively recent; in fact, the first definition dates back to 1990 and was proposed by the American psychologists Peter Salovey and John D. Mayer. Despite this, the concept of emotional intelligence began to take hold and become "famous" only between 1995 and 1996, following the publication of the book "Emotional Intelligence: What it is and why it can make us happy", by the author and science journalist Daniel Goleman.

Following the publication of Goleman's book, the concept of emotional intelligence took shape and became an object of study both in the psychological field and in the corporate organization. As we will see in the course of this chapter, in fact, according to Goleman's conception, emotional intelligence is a fundamental aspect for success in the field of business and leadership.

The transformations undergone by the concept of emotional intelligence over the years have led to the creation by psychologists and scholars of the sector of different theoretical models of EI, corresponding to equally different definitions and characteristics.

What is Emotional Intelligence?

Emotional intelligence can be described as the ability of an individual to recognize, discriminate and identify, to label appropriately and, consequently, to manage their emotions and those of others in order to achieve certain goals.

ASSERTIVE COMMUNICATION

Free Yourself

In truth, the definition of emotional intelligence has undergone several changes over the years and its meaning can take on different shades depending on the type of conception that one has of this ability to identify and manage one's own and others' emotions.

Emotional intelligence is also known as emotional quotient (EQ), emotional intelligence quotient (EIQ) and emotional leadership (EL).

Models

Theoretical Models of Emotional Intelligence

As mentioned, the conception of emotional intelligence is not univocal, but there are several proposed theoretical models that describe its meaning and characteristics. Below are two of the main models of emotional intelligence currently in existence: that of Salovey and Mayer, and that of Goleman.

Emotional Intelligence according to Salovey and Mayer

The conception of emotional intelligence initially developed by psychologists Salovey and Mayer defined it as the ability to perceive, integrate and regulate emotions to facilitate thought and promote personal growth.

However, after conducting several researches, this definition was changed to include the ability to accurately perceive emotions, to generate and understand them, so as to reflexively regulate them in order to promote one's emotional and intellectual growth.

More specifically, according to the Salovey and Mayer model, emotional intelligence includes four different abilities:

Perception of emotions: perception of emotions is a fundamental aspect of emotional intelligence. In this case, it is understood as the ability to detect and decipher not only one's own emotions, but also those of others, on people's faces, in images (for example, in photographs), in the timbre of the voice, etc.

ASSERTIVE COMMUNICATION
Free Yourself

Use of emotions: understood as the individual's ability to exploit emotions and apply them to activities such as thinking and solving problems.

Understanding of emotions: the ability to understand emotions and to understand their variations and evolution over time.

Managing emotions: the ability to regulate one's own and others' emotions, both positive and negative, managing them in such a way as to achieve the set goals.

According to Salovey and Mayer the above abilities are closely related to each other.

How is emotional intelligence measured according to Salovey and Mayer?

The degree of emotional intelligence according to the Salovey and Mayer model is measured by the Mayer-Salovey-Caruso emotional intelligence test (also known by the acronym of MSEIT). Without going into details, we will limit ourselves to saying that this tests the individual on the aforementioned abilities that characterize emotional intelligence. Unlike the classic IQ (intelligence quotient) tests, in the MSEIT there are no objectively correct answers; this feature, however, has largely contributed to questioning the reliability of the test itself.

Emotional Intelligence according to Goleman

According to the model introduced by Goleman, emotional intelligence includes a series of skills and competences that guide the individual, especially in the field of leadership.

In detail, according to Goleman, emotional intelligence is characterized by:

Self-awareness: understood as the ability to recognize one's emotions and strengths, as well as one's limitations and weaknesses; it also

ASSERTIVE COMMUNICATION
Free Yourself

includes the ability to understand how these personal characteristics are able to influence others.

Self-regulation: describes the ability to manage one's strengths, emotions and weaknesses, adapting them to the different situations that may arise, in order to achieve goals and objectives.

Social ability: consists of the ability to manage relationships with people in order to "direct" them towards the achievement of a specific goal.

Motivation: the ability to recognize negative thoughts and turn them into positive thoughts that are able to motivate oneself and others.

Empathy: the ability to fully understand and perceive and feel the mood of other people.

According to Goleman, different emotional skills belong to each of the aforementioned characteristics, understood as the practical skills of the individual necessary for the establishment of positive relationships with others. These skills, however, are not innate, but can be learned, developed and improved in order to achieve important job and leadership performance. According to Goleman, each individual is endowed with a "general" emotional intelligence from birth and the degree of this intelligence determines the - more or less high - probability of later learning and exploiting the above emotional skills.

Goleman, therefore, makes emotional intelligence a fundamental tool in the field of job success.

How is emotional intelligence measured according to Goleman?

The emotional intelligence according to Goleman can be measured through the Emotional Competency Inventory (ECI) and the Emotional and Social Competency Inventory (ESCI), these are tools developed by Goleman himself and by Richard Eleftherios Boyatzis, professor of organizational behavior, psychology and cognitive sciences.

Furthermore, it is also possible to measure emotional intelligence through the Emotional Intelligence Appraisal. It is a type of self-assessment developed by Travis Bradberry and Jean Greaves.

ASSERTIVE COMMUNICATION
Free Yourself

Effects and Benefits of Emotional Intelligence on Daily Life

Regardless of the type of model adopted to describe traits and characteristics, the presence of a high degree of emotional intelligence - understood as the ability to correctly perceive, recognize and manage one's own and others' emotions - should theoretically bring beneficial effects in all aspects of the individual's daily life.

In detail, those with emotional intelligence should:

- Have better social relationships;
- Have better family and romantic relationships;
- Be perceived by others in a more positive way than individuals with low emotional intelligence;
- Be able to establish better relationships in the workplace than those who do not have, or have a low level, of emotional intelligence;
- Be more likely to understand themselves and make correct decisions based on both logic and emotions;
- Have a better academic performance;
- Enjoy greater psychological well-being.

Those with a good level of emotional intelligence, in fact, seem to have a greater chance of having satisfaction from their life, of having a high level of self-esteem and a lower level of insecurity. Furthermore, the presence of emotional intelligence seems to be useful in preventing wrong choices and behaviors, also related to one's health (for example, abuse of psychoactive substances and addictions to both drugs and alcohol).

An interesting study conducted in 2010 analyzed the correlation between emotional intelligence and the degree of dependence on alcohol and / or drugs. From this study it emerged that the scores obtained from the tests for the evaluation of emotional intelligence increased as the degree of dependence on the aforementioned substances decreased.

The same goes for another study conducted in 2012 that analyzed the relationship between emotional intelligence, self-esteem and marijuana addiction: subjects affected by this addiction scored exceptionally low on tests for both evaluation and self-esteem.

What Emotional Intelligence is NOT

In the light of what has been said so far, it is clear that there is no single definition of emotional intelligence and how its meaning and its applications can change according to the theoretical models taken into consideration. It is therefore not surprising that the concept of emotional intelligence is often distorted and / or misunderstood and that irrelevant meanings are attributed to it. In this regard, the psychologist John D. Mayer wanted to write a few words in an article published in an American trade magazine to specify that - contrary to what can be read in numerous articles and magazines - emotional intelligence is NOT synonymous with happiness, optimism, calm and self-control, since these are traits that may or may not belong to the personality of the individual and must not be confused with the characteristics and abilities attributed to emotional intelligence.

Being self-aware means being aware of both our feelings and our thoughts about them; especially with respect to negative feeling. Being able to say: "Well, what I'm feeling is anger ... it's anxiety ... it's pain ...", can promote a healthy control of the aforementioned feelings that allows you not to get carried away by their pressure and to look for alternative ways to manage them. According to this theory, therefore, emotions do not have a negative or positive value, but it is their management that can make them positive or negative. At the base of Goleman's emotional intelligence there are two great skills: personal

ASSERTIVE COMMUNICATION
Free Yourself

competence linked to the way we control ourselves, and social competence, linked to the way we manage relationships with others.

Self-awareness, which means self-awareness of one's emotional state, i.e. knowing how to express one's feelings openly and with assertiveness, knowing one's weaknesses and strengths, understanding what can be improved and willingly accepting constructive criticism; but being self-aware of one's abilities also means having more confidence in oneself and in the possibility of self-fulfillment.

Self-management, which concerns self-control in being able to dominate strong emotions and disturbances in order to channel them towards constructive ends, as well as the integrity that is obtained from the transparency of an authentic openness to others of one's feelings, beliefs, actions.

Empathy, i.e. the ability to perceive and recognize the feelings of others, to emotionally tune in with them and adopt their perspective.

Motivation, that is the ability to guide and encourage oneself to achieve one's goals, becoming, with commitment and positivity, the architects of one's own change.

Social skills, therefore managing emotions in relationships well and knowing how to accurately read social situations in order to effectively deal with interactions, conflicts, communication problems.

All these components allow us to always remain in contact with our emotional inner world and consequently to find harmony with ourselves, they also build the essence of the success of interpersonal relationships, the ability to read the reactions and feelings of others, skill in deflecting and resolving inevitable conflicts that arise in any human activity.

CHAPTER 6 EMOTIONAL INTELLIGENCE IN THE COUPLE

The role of emotional intelligence in the couple relationship

We can consider emotional intelligence as the ability to better live one's own emotions and those of others. Peter Salovey, an American psychologist who dealt with the topic of emotional intelligence for the first time, identifies 5 main areas:

1. Self-awareness, i.e. the recognition of one's emotions at the very moment they arise.

2. The ability to manage them rather than succumb to them.

3. Empathy, i.e. recognizing the emotions that others feel.

4. Self-motivation, which involves the ability to remain motivated in achieving one's goals despite the failures and frustrations that may arise along the way, and is therefore supported by an adequate dose of optimism and hope and, finally;

5. Social competence, that is to say the ability to manage interpersonal relationships and therefore to dominate the emotions of others.

ASSERTIVE COMMUNICATION
Free Yourself

Having made this premise, we can understand how important the ability to exercise adequate emotional control, first of all of one's emotions, is also in the couple relationship. Over the years there has been a notable increase in divorces. US research has shown that couples who married in 1970 were 50% likely to separate, while couples who married in 1990 were up to 67% likely to. Undoubtedly, this change is due to the lesser influence of social pressures that once "forced" even unhappy couples to stay together.

This means that the glue that keeps a marriage alive today is emotional bonds. It is no longer external social or cultural rules that weld the union but something personal, profound, interior that becomes the real foundation of marriage. Sophisticated studies on couple bonds and on the behaviors that destroy them, have shown that couple difficulties originate in childhood, from the differences between the emotional reality of girls and that of boys: We observe a different approach of parents towards male children and towards daughters: for example, parents tend to discuss emotions more with girls than with boys and, when they play with daughters, mothers express a wider range of emotions.

This would predispose girls, once adults, to enter marriage with greater emotional competence than men, a greater ability to understand emotions expressed in non-verbal language, a greater propensity to express feelings and a greater ability to manage them.

The effects of this different approach are observed in the interactions between children. As they grow older, males tend to seek competition in their games, while females mostly play in small groups in which they favor cooperation and intimacy. This makes men and women expect different things from a conversation: men talk about facts; women talk about emotions.

Men, as their marriage or relationship grows stronger, are less and less willing to talk because they consider intimacy as something to do with their wives: go shopping or plan vacations. Women, on the other hand, consider communication essential.

ASSERTIVE COMMUNICATION

Free Yourself

Research by Ruben C. Gur of Pennsylvania University's school of medicine found that men downplay emotions and have a harder time recognizing non-verbal emotional cues. For a man to be able to recognize his wife's sadness, she must be very depressed!

Women dwell more on their relationship problems, while men have a rosier view of their marriage.

Beyond the problems that may exist in a couple, what matters for the duration of a marriage is the way in which the couple deals with them.

Marriage: advice for use: women tend to complain more, to recognize the presence of a problem even where there are no problems for the man; it is important then that when women scold their partners, they just scold the wrong action (protest) not the person (criticize). Ex: "You left your clothes on the floor. When you behave like this you make me nervous because I always try to keep the house tidy and I don't feel understood". The protest is directed at the husband's action and explains how this action made his wife feel. It is not an attack on the husband. The criticism: "You still left your clothes on the floor. I've told you a thousand times and you don't understand anything. You're a good-for-nothing slob".

Personal criticism is an attack on the person who, as a result, will feel humiliation and shame and will react with a defensive response rather than trying to make things better. For their part, men should:

- Not avoid conflict;
- Consider the woman's complaint as an act of love in order to make the relationship work;
- If the resentment continues over time, sooner or later anger explodes and the woman can attack the man "heavily". In these cases, the man must understand that this reaction indicates the intensity with which the woman feels that problem;
- Avoid short cuts, by giving solutions: the man who is always rather practical and less emotional, in the face of a woman's complaint often provides ready-to-use solutions, that most of the time only increase the sensation of the woman feeling

ASSERTIVE COMMUNICATION

Free Yourself

misunderstood. The woman just needs to feel that her feelings are understood even though the man may not agree with her, what matters is that he is listening to her.

There are repair mechanisms that prevent an argument from leading to a violent quarrel, for example: avoiding rambling, empathizing with your partner, calming tension. It is important not to dwell too much on the problems often subject to conflict in couples (children, economic problems etc..). John Gottman, an internationally renowned psychologist in the field of emotional intelligence, argues that empathy, the ability to listen to the other, to calm them down are all fundamental skills for the fights within the couple to be positive and constructive.

To calm down, it can be useful during an argument to pause a few minutes when you notice that the intensity of anger increases: a walk, aerobic exercise, a relaxation exercise may be enough to regain emotional control. When negative thoughts about your partner start to arise during an argument it can be helpful to replace them with positive memories, for example a wife who thinks of her husband, "still he doesn't even listen to me, he doesn't care about me", may try to remember the times when the husband proved otherwise. A very useful technique is mirroring: when a partner expresses the protest the other repeats it with his own words trying to grasp the underlying feelings; this creates emotional harmony between the couple and avoids conflict, has a calming effect on the partner, who feels understood. These are just some of the useful tips to improve communication within the couple and to consolidate the relationship. These are skills that are difficult to put into practice from one day to the next, so they require training. You have to try, try, try, so that like all the things you learn, they become habits. Educating emotional intelligence from an early age would be the best way to positive and constructive adult relationships and, probably a fulfilled life. It is still possible for people of all ages to acquire the skills necessary for adequate awareness and management of emotions.

ASSERTIVE COMMUNICATION

Free Yourself

5 Emotional intelligence exercises

In 5 steps we can improve our emotional intelligence and live better with ourselves and with others.

Emotional intelligence can be defined as the ability to know one's own and others' emotions, to regulate them in a functional and positive way, to motivate oneself, to assume an empathic attitude both towards oneself and in relationships. It is a fundamental characteristic of everyday life and must be trained and improved from the first years of life. It should be present in school and work contexts, as a constant that animates the actions of each and the group.

To train emotional intelligence, it is necessary to act on what scholars define its sub-components.

Improve your awareness. Increasing self-awareness is the first step to increasing emotional intelligence because through greater knowledge of one's own experience, emotions and feelings, it is possible to learn to respect, regulate and control them in a functional way. To improve self-awareness, it is important to question oneself, set goals, ask oneself what one wants and expects from oneself and from situations and at the end of the day reliving what has been done and observing oneself from the outside to understand one's reactions and ways of being. Training must be constant and start from asking oneself about what motivated one's actions, and understanding how to modify or strengthen it over time.

Regulate your emotions. Self-regulation means the ability to regulate one's emotions and channel them correctly before acting and reacting to different circumstances. The ability to self-regulate passes through the awareness of one's own experience and the ability to pay attention to it in the here and now. Relaxation, meditation and mindfulness techniques are useful for increasing the ability to be present in the here

ASSERTIVE COMMUNICATION
Free Yourself

and now, and reduce excessive emotional activation, restoring a state of stillness, monitoring and control of one's own experience.

Be empathetic. Empathy is commonly known as the ability to put yourself in the shoes of others, or to understand the emotions of others and act by considering and monitoring them. Increasing empathic abilities through the constant attempt to understand the state of others, and placing one's attention on it increases one's emotional intelligence, allowing one to regulate one's actions and make sense even to the apparently unfair or meaningless behavior of others. This will inevitably affect one's relationships enriching them with the ability to monitor one's own behavior and adapt it to different external realities and to others.

Be motivated. Another important aspect of emotional intelligence is the ability to motivate oneself, or to maintain an optimal level of activation and functional to the achievement of set goals within your reach, achievable and simple. Planning one step at a time, learning to rejoice in successes and react to failures with determination, are good skills at the basis of emotional intelligence because they allow you to welcome your own and others' experiences and abilities, to respect it and to act accordingly.

Increase your social skills. Finally, there are social skills, because emotional intelligence is strongly intersected with social living and relationships. Working for the development of social and prosocial skills, which take into account the context, one's own characteristics and those of others, acting with respect and understanding, is fundamental to improving the emotional skills of the individual and of the group and reciprocal action. It is therefore important to learn to manage relationships, to react to stress and difficulties in a functional way, which takes into account different points of view and different opportunities. Emotional intelligence is a fundamental characteristic of everyday life because it conveys one's actions and reactions, influencing relationships in a more or less positive or negative way and therefore social life, as well as one's own experience and well-being.

CHAPTER 7 WHAT EMPATHY IS AND HOW TO DEVELOP IT FOR BETTER COMMUNICATION

All of us are endowed with a precious gift, which allows us to get in touch with the emotions of the other; this gift is called empathy. Through empathy we have the opportunity to identify with the other person's emotional experience, to grasp the most significant part of the message he addresses to us.

What is empathy?

Empathy is the heart of emotional intelligence, an essential skill that improves communication and involves the ability to experience the feelings of another person without losing our identity.

"Through empathy we can enter into a deep connection with those around us"

Empathy is the human quality behind empathic listening. The latter is the typically assertive way of giving due attention to the message the other wants to get to us.

While it is a human skill, not everyone develops it easily. There are those who are very empathetic by nature, without too much effort. And there are those who need to work harder to be able to establish such a connection.

Does it happen to you too, that you have the feeling that you are not being listened to?

A frequent problem with listening is that, while the other is speaking, we remember something else that has to do with what he is telling us, and we are all caught up in having "our say" at the first pause. Then

ASSERTIVE COMMUNICATION

Free Yourself

there are certain animated conversations, in which some take away the word from the others, but in which little is listened to.

EXAMPLE

Has it ever happened to you to tell something personal and to be interrupted by your interlocutor to report a similar experience? The classic case ... "This morning I woke up with a migraine that didn't ..." - he interrupts you and begins with "Oh my God, I'm tormented by morning headaches ... you have no idea ..."

You can "listen" in different ways, here are some examples.

Listen but ignore;

Pretend to listen ("Yes", "Ah", "I understand ...");

Selective listening (choosing to listen only to what you want to hear);

Listening carefully without evaluations (for example, taking notes during a conference);

Empathic listening (with the intention of understanding the other party).

The essence of empathic listening is understanding others from two fundamental points of view: the intellectual (understanding what they think), the emotional (understanding what they feel).

How to become an empathic person

Would you like to be heard or to listen deeply? Try to think about what happens to you when you feel that someone is genuinely trying to understand your point of view. Is it not true that you recognize his openness and that you are more willing to find an agreement with your interlocutor? If you want to learn empathic listening, reflect on these tips that you find in the following paragraphs.

ASSERTIVE COMMUNICATION

Free Yourself

1) Pay attention to what others are saying

The empathic person listens to every word in a conversation, but above all he listens by showing real attention. And he doesn't listen to answer, but shows real interest in what one has to say.

It may seem like a minor thing to you, but listening carefully is a gift to the interlocutor, a difficult skill to adopt. Usually, you listen to formulate an answer and retort. The problem is that the connections you form with others aren't always that solid.

If you want to be an empathic person you will have to be actively listening to the other person's needs, trying to enter the world of the other, even if you do not share it. It is only in this way that you will be able to become aware of what is not being said, that is, the worries and fears of the other.

2) Enhance curiosity

As children we are taught that asking too many questions is rude, but the reality is very different.

While there are things that are best not to ask, unless there is a certain level of confidence, that doesn't mean you should never ask questions.

If you want to be an empathic person, you have to get carried away with experiences and whatever knowledge the other person has. And there's no better way to connect with someone than by asking questions about their life and showing interest in what they have to tell you.

So next time you talk to someone, ask them about their interests, dreams and goals. This exercise will help you develop empathy because it forces you to see reality from the other person's perspective.

3) Learn to manage your emotions

ASSERTIVE COMMUNICATION

Free Yourself

Obviously, you know that you cannot control the events that happen to you, much less the actions or thoughts of others, but you have full control over the way you react to them and the ability to express and communicate your feelings and emotions.

By putting yourself in the shoes of an observer, you will be able to look at your feelings with the necessary detachment and this will benefit the relationship with others; when you may happen to "collide" with another person, it will be easier for you to argue with this person without letting anger and resentment take over and stiffen you. Take a few deep breaths and bring back control over your emotions to handle the situation more constructively for both of you.

4) Learn to recognize the wealth of others

Every relationship, from the most superficial to the most intimate and profound, is an opportunity to learn and enrich oneself. It is an opportunity to exchange opinions, consider a new point of view, give birth to new ideas, improve ourselves as people. No one is ever a waste of time, quite the contrary.

Try to see other people as an opportunity to shed some light on yourself, another voice you haven't heard yet.

5) Learn to put aside judgments

When you actively listen to the other person's needs, you have to put aside judgments, emotional traps that distance you from people and prevent you from truly knowing them. You must learn to trust others and of course receive respect and trust in turn. But how does criticism and judgment give rise to respect and trust? Who likes to be criticized and judged?

Sometimes you don't even notice that you are judging and how this is limiting your world view and ruining your relationships. As human

ASSERTIVE COMMUNICATION

Free Yourself

beings we have the power to talk well or badly about ourselves and others.

What words come out of your mouth? Are they words (and thoughts) of esteem, approval, encouragement or judgment and criticism? Do they bring you closer or distance you from others?

6) Don't impose your point of view

When someone is opening up to you and asking you for advice, you may fall into the temptation to "step into the chair" and say how they should behave, following your map of thoughts, rather than that of the other person. It is much more rewarding and constructive to actively listen and let the other person find the best solution for them. How much do you support others in finding their solutions?

Learn to question yourself

An empathic person, when he talks to someone who does not share his lifestyle, does not refuse to listen to him; and this obviously does not mean accepting his opinion as absolute truth. He listens, asks and questions himself.

You must learn that there is no one solution for everything and that everyone has their reasons. Learn to exchange opinions in a constructive way. At the end of the discussion, maybe you can change your opinion or maybe have more clarity on certain opinions. Of course, you do not have to do it just to be nice. If you change your mind, do it because you really believe in it.

To be an empathic person, it's important to engage with people who think differently from you on certain topics. Listen to their opinions and express your ideas. The most important thing in this process is not to try to get anyone to accept your ideas, just listen.

ASSERTIVE COMMUNICATION
Free Yourself

7) Learn to measure your language

Speaking well is as important as knowing how to listen. To become an empathic person, one must value language; words are a weapon that can save or sink someone, so be very careful what you say.

Sometimes you can make the mistake of underestimating the difference between helping and ordering. When talking to someone who is down in the dumps, say things like, "I can't imagine it", or, "How can I help you?" Rather than saying: "Come on, you're exaggerating", or, "Don't worry", The person will understand that you are really trying to understand him and that you are not judging him.

8) Don't treat everyone equally

The empathic person does not treat all people equally, they know that not everyone likes to be treated the same way. Learn to put aside pride and accept that there is more than one way to be right. Remember, we are all different and we all have different needs.

Do not label someone for their attitude or experience, without thinking that they have a history behind them that influences their actions. Perhaps that experience is insignificant to you, but to the other it can carry a great deal of emotional weight. This doesn't mean you can't express decisions or what you want. On the contrary: explain what you feel or want, but with respect to those in front of you.

For example, if your partner is unable to say "I love you" this does not mean that he is not in love with you; it is certainly not this attitude that can determine whether a person loves you or not! Don't expect me to tell you what you want to hear; don't extort phrases from him that you love to hear. Rather, try to understand the cause of his difficulty. Let him know that you would like to hear certain words but without expecting to.

9) Learn to recognize your emotions

ASSERTIVE COMMUNICATION
Free Yourself

Emotions are important because they are the bridge between who you are and what is important to you. When someone is sharing their emotions, whether positive or negative, listen. By doing so, you allow the other person to unload and feel heard and understood. Consequently, the positive emotions will increase and the negative ones will slowly go away. Think about your interactions: how much do you encourage elaboration and clarification with others? How well do you recognize their and your emotions?

REMEMBER...

This is not an innate ability, but an art that you can easily learn. Unfortunately, not everyone has had a good emotional upbringing (not for this we must blame the parents) but it does not mean that it is too late to learn. From now on you can put into practice the advice I just suggested.

ASSERTIVE COMMUNICATION
Free Yourself

CHAPTER 8 THE RIGHT TO SAY NO

If there is one thing, we hardly express, it is rejection. Therefore, we are often perceived as nice people, very brave... but without personality. It's not about becoming selfish or stopping helping people. It is simply about doing what we really want and without feeling guilty about our decisions. Say no... it exists.

In the life we live every day, it is necessary, for example, to know how to reject a boy's unwelcome advances, to say no to a salesman after his five-minute speech about the benefits of the revolutionary vacuum cleaner, or to admit to your boss that this additional task cannot be done without extra resources. Furthermore, in this regard, it is important to clarify that there is not only yes and no. There is also negotiation... especially with the boss ...

Let's analyze in practice why you can say a sharp NO:

- If you don't want to do something, say NO, and not YES. It is your right as an individual.

- There is no need to find justifications in all cases. Even if being diplomatic with the boss enters the broad sphere of relationship management and a possible request for a future increase, the refusal to the seller is your right. Above all because, in the event of silence, you would face a further "attack" by the seller, who will move on to the next phase to achieve his noble goal: the sale! My friend Riccardo in 1994, when he went into a clothes shop in the center of Rome to have a look and in front of him, he saw a beautiful saleswoman, he no longer understood anything and promptly went out full of useless purchases! Now he has learned to say the firm NO!

ASSERTIVE COMMUNICATION
Free Yourself

- If negotiation is the best solution, start by sharply rejecting the proposal before starting the negotiation. If you go the other way around, you would start at a disadvantage.

Here is now a five-step method for you to say NO. However, in most cases, the five steps are interchangeable:

1 - Start by saying NO in a clear and precise way. "No, I don't want to buy anything."

2 - Articulate if you need the sentence in the negative: "As I told you, my answer is NO."

3 - Show empathy to help your rejection. "I think you have to work hard to sell vacuum cleaners and I'm sorry, but I don't care." If necessary, also underline it in broken record mode "I don't care, thanks. I don't care, thanks!"

4 - If you argue with someone and they insist on convincing you, express your negative emotions. "This discussion is starting to tire me and it bothers me that you continue to insist".

5 - Finally, if someone wants to convince you with a sense of guilt, it's time to understand what is good for yourself, and if what is good for you is to close the door in his face, just do it! The sense of guilt is created by us and used by our mind to hurt us: paradoxical, but it is so!

ASSERTIVE COMMUNICATION

Free Yourself

All these aspects must be used according to the person in front of you. In the human sciences there can be no objectivity. Sometimes being too firm and terse in denial can lead to you not getting consent. For example, if you are looking for a way to get something, it is much easier to get it by providing a "why" you want it!

Saying no is sometimes difficult but there are some little tricks that help us do this without sounding rude and insensitive.

Saying no is always very complicated, yet it is one of the most important skills if you want to live a life over which you have full control and want to have the time to achieve any of our goals (work, family, friendship).

The fear of saying no is defeated first of all with the awareness that saying "no" is your right. Your time is yours, and you should decide what to do with it.

That is why I have decided to talk about this topic, which I am sure will be a further weapon in the briefcase of any person, interested in persuasion or sales. Or it can help us untangle ourselves in the maze of the various proposals that continually come to us.

Always give strong motivation. Never indicate a false motivation that can be easily dismantled or unmasked. In this way you will risk passing for a liar and untrustworthy person. For example: suppose a friend invites you to the cinema, but you don't want to go because you don't like the movie. Instead of saying no with this reason, you use the excuse that you have small children and cannot leave them alone. The friend might say: "Ah but don't worry, my mother is taking care of my little ones, so we can leave yours with her too." In two seconds, his answer dismantles your excuse and so you have no more reason not to go.

"At the moment I have other priorities". If you have something more important to do, simply to say no without saying no, you have to say that you have other priorities. This will also serve to block the other person from making other requests to you in the immediate future. If you want to be even more convincing, then share your schedule with the other person so that they see with their own eyes how busy you are.

ASSERTIVE COMMUNICATION
Free Yourself

Ask as many questions as possible. When your intention is to say no to the proposal being made to you, asking a lot of questions could shift the other person's attention to the wrong strategies, goals, and motivations of that proposal. Or the fact that that idea isn't quite right.

"I would love to but ...". If you like the idea they propose, but you really can't, then mask saying no in this way "I would love to but ...". This will make you look really believable and convincing, because you are rejecting something you would like to do.

Say no without saying no

"Give me a moment to think about it." Sometimes we don't know how to say yes or no right away. In this case it is good to ask for a few minutes to reflect and organize all your commitments. This method is a similar no in the short term, but you need to take time and make all the necessary assessments.

"I'll put it on my Good Ideas List." You should have a list, where you write down the things you want to realize someday. By showing that you put it on that list, you will give the correct impression, that is, that the idea will not be forgotten. Therefore, even if you have not accepted, it may be sufficient to gratify the person making the proposal. A no with class.

"I do not know. But maybe we can... ". This is where the face-to-face technique comes into play. With this method you will say no to a request but, immediately afterwards, you will propose, in order not to disappoint them, another smaller one or more distant in time. This method works well, but only use it if in the future you really want to live up to this commitment and not have to use "no" again.

ASSERTIVE COMMUNICATION
Free Yourself

4 SIMPLE TIPS FOR ACTION

Be firm. If you give the impression that you will think about it, others will continue to make unwanted proposals to you.

Don't say a yes that is a no. Do not accept a proposal thinking that anyway you go home and let them know that you regret it. It's a way of doing things that won't show you in a good light.

You don't owe anybody explanations. Remember that you don't always have to give a reason. "I have too many commitments" or "I can't cope with the schedules" are just fine.

Work out. Start saying no today by following these instructions. Especially when you don't know what to do or when you don't feel like doing something. You will be surprised to see that people will react better than you think to the answers described above.

ASSERTIVE COMMUNICATION

Free Yourself

CHAPTER 9 THE IMPORTANCE OF SETTING BOUNDARIES

Think about important themes in relationships: romantic and platonic. What comes to your mind?

Many of us would say loyalty, trust, communication, happiness, respect etc. But one thing that I feel overlooked is borders.

Healthy boundaries in a relationship - whether it's with yourself or others - or whether it's romantic or not, helps us with all of those aforementioned themes.

In my previous job as a psychologist assistant, I have worked with many families to improve their boundaries to help them support, trust and communicate better with their loved ones.

It is an essential pillar that allows us to have a good mix of dependence and independence in relationships.

That said, I'll walk you through three simple ways to set healthy boundaries that can have a big impact on your relationships.

1. **Be aware of your limitations**

Many of us don't know how to set healthy boundaries because we aren't aware of what we find acceptable or not.

It is practically impossible to establish a border without knowing this.

For example, we could tell our partner that we agree that they can use our phone whenever they want, but we don't really feel comfortable.

ASSERTIVE COMMUNICATION
Free Yourself

There's nothing wrong with that - you might plan a surprise for them so you don't want them to use your phone. However, without having that awareness of knowing that you are not comfortable with them using the phone as and when they want, it makes it difficult to establish the line in the first place.

Instead, opening our awareness and knowledge to what we are actually comfortable and uncomfortable with is an essential step in establishing a healthy boundary.

2. How to implement it:

Explore your limits by examining past experiences: what did you find that you didn't like and what were you most comfortable with? This is an easy way to understand your limitations.

Psychology professor, Dr. Mariana Bockarova, says: "Create a 'boundary table' that delineates each boundary for each category of relationship and fill it with boundary criteria with which you feel comfortable and safe, and viceversa". This boundary card allows you to see your limits in front of you, drawing awareness to them. You can then adapt your limits to what you are most comfortable with.

The mental distress caused by boundaries that conflict with our values is so painful.

But why do we set boundaries in the first place that conflict with our values? Three reasons come to mind:

We don't know what our true values are.

We don't want to be seen as harsh.

We are more interested in pleasing the other person, so we create these pleasant boundaries for people, even if they go against our values.

This is because our values give us purpose and motivate our actions and attitudes. So, if we create boundaries that match our values, it can

ASSERTIVE COMMUNICATION
Free Yourself

provide us with a broader direction and mean that our actions match our belief systems, which will always make us feel better.

How to implement:

Find out your values first: a short exercise is to identify three values and affirm them by writing about the value or speaking aloud (to yourself or someone else). If you find it difficult to process that value, chances are it's not that important to you.

Stanford psychologist Dr. Kelly McGonigal says, "Describe why this value is important to you and / or your family or community. You could also write about how you express this value in your daily life. If you are facing a difficult experience or decision, you may want to write about how this value might guide or support you. This helps you understand what your true values are.

Now set your limits: because you understand your values and why they matter, setting limits becomes easier. My value is honesty with friends and family, so I have a limit to make sure I'm honest with them, but they are honest with me too.

Find out your values first. Hence, setting boundaries becomes easier and healthier.

3. Act on your boundaries

Establishing a healthy boundary is not just about creating it. It also involves you acting on it.

This is because it strengthens your belief and gives others a message that you are not a push-over.

It's also extremely healthy to act on a boundary because when you don't, the other person can become disrespectful and think they can get away with anything. For instance:

ASSERTIVE COMMUNICATION

Free Yourself

If a student doesn't do their homework on time and the teacher lets them go, the student might try their luck again because she might think her teacher will let her off the hook again.

Also, if other students see it, they might try their luck too. So starts a dangerous cycle where people will test the teacher's boundaries more frequently.

How to implement:

Practice saying no: this does not have to be related to a boundary, you could practice by saying no to your friends when they ask you to come and have coffee. It will help you feel comfortable saying no by helping you act on your limits.

Develop assertiveness - the tip above will help you with this. But you can also get more assertive by doing things like asking for a different table in a restaurant. Or, simply disagree with someone's opinion (but with respect). Again, it's all about getting comfortable with being assertive which will make acting on your boundaries a breeze.

Don't give long explanations when enforcing your boundaries - Psychotherapist Sharon Martin says "This type of behavior undermines your authority and gives the impression that you are doing something wrong that requires apology or justification." Keeping it short, sweet, and simple when it comes to taking action on your boundary is a great way to help strengthen your boundary.

Setting boundaries is a fundamental pillar in our relationships. It is what helps us communicate better, be happy and develop trust with other people.

Setting boundaries doesn't have to be difficult. Instead, these three tricks can help you set healthier boundaries:

Be aware of your limitations.

Set limits in line with your values.

ASSERTIVE COMMUNICATION
Free Yourself

Act on your borders.

These three tricks will first help you identify what you are comfortable and uncomfortable with. It will therefore help you to set limits that do not lead to any mental discomfort. And finally, it will help you develop ways on how to act on them.

ASSERTIVE COMMUNICATION

Free Yourself

CHAPTER 10 HOW TO OVERCOME YOUR OWN INSECURITY

We often read phrases and texts that motivate us to increase self-confidence, but rarely do they explain "how to do it", rather they tell us "What we must do".

The theory is very important, but practice is more important. It is a good thing to understand the origin of the problem, find an answer to why we are insecure or understand what we need to do. However, we do not always have the tools and practical exercises that really help us to increase our self-confidence.

Perhaps little is said about the practical aspect because each person is unique. What works for someone may not work for someone else. We can share a technique that has worked for us, but perhaps those who try to put it into practice will not see results or improvements.

We are unique, each of us has our own experiences and beliefs which, however similar they may be, are very personal.

What should an insecure person do?

An insecure person must work on their self-esteem to strengthen it. Most insecurities are associated with low self-esteem, an exaggerated fear of suffering, of not being accepted, of making a fool of oneself, etc.

Instead of opening their eyes and recognizing that they have low self-esteem, many people choose to wear a mask, they deceive themselves by creating false self-esteem.

ASSERTIVE COMMUNICATION

Free Yourself

You've probably read lots of tips and tricks to increase self-esteem. You have to love yourself, be flexible, value your qualities and strengths, think above all about yourself and less about the judgment of others, etc.

All this is true, but many think: "I know I have to value myself more, the problem is that I don't really think I'm that special, so what do I do? How can I enhance my qualities more?"

Discover and enhance your qualities

To change the personal opinion that each of us has of himself, it is not enough to repeat positive phrases. We can say to ourselves every day "I'm special", "Courage! You are worth a lot!" But while this type of encouragement can increase motivation and positivity, it is equally true that it has a fleeting, momentary effect.

If we really want to change, we need to change our way of thinking.

If you too are insecure and have to write down your strengths and weaknesses, probably the column of defects would be longer. And this is where the problem lies, we are what we think of ourselves.

If you don't think you are special, your confidence will not increase. To strengthen your self-confidence, you need to look at yourself from a different perspective, much more positive, confident and realistic.

Begin to have more confidence in yourself with this exercise.

How can we enhance ourselves when we actually think we are not so special? If we underestimate ourselves, it will be difficult to become more confident.

Each person excels at something. Some discover it faster than others and do not stop empowering and showing the world their qualities, while someone else fails to identify his strengths and continues to compare himself to others he considers better.

ASSERTIVE COMMUNICATION

Free Yourself

A footballer has millions of fans who admire him because he is good at playing football. If the player had not enhanced his sporting quality and had instead dedicated himself to any university career that was not in his heart, he would not have been able to take advantage of his qualities and probably would not be so appreciated.

If you don't find your strong point, or are unable to look at yourself with positive eyes, you will freeze. Insecure people are usually perfectionists and tend to be very hard on themselves.

What is a defect for some is a virtue for others? It all depends on the direction and perspective you want to take. We suggest that you change your point of view regarding some flaws you think you have.

Consider, for example, a shy person who sees this aspect of her character as a flaw and thinks that no one will ever want to be in a relationship with her. For sure I have also known a person like that.

A person who, according to her, will never meet a partner because she is attracted to self-confident people who would never choose to be with someone insecure. An adamant person, who never changes her mind because she thinks it's impossible. One day, this person decided to try to get to know the people she is attracted to, even though she is convinced that she will be rejected.

You know someone who makes you change your way of seeing things. What she saw as a defect, the other person considers a virtue, that is, he feels that shy people have something special. Most insecure people have great sensitivity, a rich inner world, and usually take great care of their partner.

All people, without exception, have a positive side and a negative side. You can make sure that what you consider a flaw, you try to turn into a positive aspect.

CHAPTER 11 NON-VERBAL COMMUNICATION

Fundamental rules of non-verbal communication.

It is impossible not to communicate because every behavior is a direct communication to others. Every communication has a content aspect and a relationship aspect. Through every communication, even the apparently most objective one, not only data and facts are expressed, but also relationship modalities. We communicate both through language and through the body. These two communication modes express different responses to the subject. Language expresses the rational reaction to an event, the body the instinctive one.

What is non-verbal communication?

Non-verbal communication is all that is beyond words. One can speak, in general, of body language, but the tone of voice, pauses in conversation, interpersonal distance, clothing and many other elements are also part of non-verbal communication. Non-verbal communication is a primitive and instinctive mode of communication, present in all evolved animals. In fact, the signs of aggression, submission, courtship of various animal species are well known. Man has kept this type of communication as a reminder of the distant past, but he has also enriched his non-verbal repertoire with the contribution of culture, for example by codifying new gestures (the handshake in the first place).

What does non-verbal communication express?

Non-verbal communication expresses our emotions and the relationship you want to have with the interlocutor on a deep emotional level. Verbal communication, on the other hand, expresses contents and facts and the type of relationship that one wants to assume explicitly and consciously with the interlocutor.

Characteristics of non-verbal communication.

Generally speaking, non-verbal communication is faster, less aware and less controllable than verbal communication. Non-verbal reactions to an event tend to be immediate and to occur before it can be rationally evaluated. Often, we are aware only of our rational assessment of a fact and not of our instinctive one.

Consequently, we are not aware of the meaning of our non-verbal expressions. Non-verbal communication is innate, verbal communication must be learned. For example, the expression and understanding of emotions through facial expressions are skills already present in babies of a few months.

Non-verbal communication is difficult to control, also because its meaning is very often unconscious. However, if we become aware of the meaning of some attitudes, we can, in part, control and modify them. Attempting to control non-verbal communication, however, can be a double-edged sword, because it can, in some cases, give a feeling of falsity to the observer. In general, it is easier to positively control interpersonal distance, physical contact, direction of gaze, pauses.

More difficult to control are gestures, body position, facial expressions and tone of voice. On the other hand, it is almost impossible to control the physiological reactions, on which the "lie detector" is based.

It has been experimentally demonstrated that non-verbal communication is not only capable of expressing emotions but also of inducing them. In other words, if you start smiling, unless you have serious reasons to be sad, after a few minutes you really feel a little happier and interpret events in a more positive way.

ASSERTIVE COMMUNICATION
Free Yourself

What if there is a dissonance between verbal and non-verbal communication?

Non-verbal reactions can be different, even completely opposite to what is expressed verbally. In this case, it will be the non-verbal communication that is predominant and redefine the meaning of the words, which can, for example, take on an ironic tone.

How important is non-verbal communication?

It has been experimentally shown that the first impression we make of a person is influenced 90% by his non-verbal communication and only 10% by what he says.

Elements of non-verbal communication

Non-verbal communication includes everything that goes beyond verbal communication. Numerous elements make up non-verbal communication, analyzed below.

TONE OF VOICE

The tone of the voice provides important indications as to how the communication should be interpreted. It can be questioning, ironic, sarcastic, aggressive ...

PAUSES IN COMMUNICATION

Silences are usually a source of embarrassment in a conversation. However, it is often advisable to tolerate them.

We must learn to distinguish between the silence due to a moment of reflection and therefore necessary to the interlocutor, the silence that intends to communicate something and the silence that indicates, instead, a closure of communication. The first must be tolerated, the

ASSERTIVE COMMUNICATION

Free Yourself

second is often used as a request for help, closeness and support, while the last must signal a relational problem in progress. Useful indicators for interpreting silence can be obtained from non-verbal communication.

FACIAL MIMICRY

There are particular facial configurations attributable to some primary emotions, which seem to be innate and independent of culture. The generally recognized primary emotions are happiness, surprise, fear, sadness, anger, disgust.

DIRECTION OF GAZE

It is always good to look your interlocutor in the eye.

Avoiding the gaze can be a sign of disinterest, shyness and closure or rejection of the current relationship.

Persistently looking a person in the eye, especially if this is done by remaining silent for long moments, creates anxiety and discomfort in the interlocutor and gives the impression of being in front of a "strange" or "deviant" person. This behavior typically communicates keen emotional and sexual interest, or competition or challenge.

If you are dealing with a group, it is important that the gaze is turned, alternatively, to all the members of the group.

GESTURES

Hand gestures can have different meanings depending on whether or not they involve touching small objects or parts of your body.

The gestures not directed towards one's body serve to emphasize verbal communication and have an oratory value. They are generally implemented consciously to seek the interlocutor's consent and can therefore be useful for attracting attention.

Gestures that involve touching one's body, such as scratching, fiddling with fingers, rings, necklaces, generally indicate embarrassment and are usually unconscious.

ASSERTIVE COMMUNICATION

Free Yourself

STANCE

From the position of the body, it is possible to deduce the attitude towards the interlocutor.

The torso leaning forward and the legs and arms slightly open are indicators of availability and openness. Instead, the torso and body moved backwards, the arms folded and, to a lesser extent, the legs crossed, indicate closure, refusal and disinterest.

Clasping the hands behind the back instead signals security and superiority, real or ostentatious.

PERSONAL SPACE

The physical distance between two people has deep emotional values.

In fact, each of us tends to divide the space into four areas:

Intimate area: up to 30 cm around the subject. Only those who are affectionately close to us can enter this area without creating annoyance or embarrassment.

Personal area: approximately from 30 cm to 1 meter. It is the area used for social relations and friendship.

Social Zone: approximately from 1 to 3 meters. This area is usually dedicated to communications with acquaintances, colleagues and with all people who do not know each other well.

Public area: over 3 meters. It is the sphere in which we move at ease when surrounded by strangers.

In situations in which unwanted contact is required, for example in a lift or tram, certain behaviors are usually carried out with the function of maintaining a certain privacy. We tend not to talk; we avoid staring into people's eyes and we limit facial expressions.

PHYSICAL CONTACT

Physical contact between people is culturally regulated.

ASSERTIVE COMMUNICATION

Free Yourself

In almost all cultures it is widely used within the family unit. Also, in this case there are precise rules that establish which parts of the body can be touched and by whom.

In Western culture, touching a stranger is only allowed in situations of greeting, introduction and farewell. In cultures such as Japanese and English, touching strangers is almost completely avoided, while in African and Arab cultures, physical contact is used often and in many circumstances.

It is always advisable to respect cultural conventions, in order to avoid creating embarrassment in others.

PHYSIOLOGICAL REACTIONS

Rapid heartbeat, sweating, shortness of breath, blushing, blanching are just some of the possible physiological reactions caused by a strong emotion, often of fear or shame.

Sometimes manifesting some of these signals is natural; showing these reactions often reveals insecurity and poor self-control. Never showing any physiological reaction conveys coldness and a lack of spontaneity.

Non-verbal communication includes all aspects of a communicative exchange that does not concern the purely semantic level of the message, so it concerns body language, an unspoken communication between people.

Verbal messages are integrated with gestures, postures, body orientation, interpersonal distance, facial expressions, tone, rhythm and timbre of the voice.

The objectives of non-verbal communication are:

- Interpret the interlocutor's body language,
- Manage your own NVC (non-verbal communication).

ASSERTIVE COMMUNICATION

Free Yourself

Can body language help in interpersonal relationships?

Alterations in the tone of the voice and contractions in posture greatly affect the impact that is obtained with people, especially when the interlocutor is shy or unsure of himself.

According to Professor of Psychology, Albert Mehrabian, in communication, words represent 7%, paraverbal communication 38% and non-verbal communication 55%.

In this study, the importance of tone of voice (positive, negative or neutral) was compared to the content of words spoken by two different individuals. In the second part of the research, the reaction to the tone of voice of some people who pronounced the word "maybe" was analyzed, presenting photos with random facial expressions of photo models.

This explains that communication is the main tool by which one comes into contact with others. In fact, the possibility of communicating different experiences is given by facial expressions, gestures and postures with which safety, trust and authority are emphasized, or the opposite.

There are some signals that are more easily controlled and some totally involuntary signals.

Generally, the signals of the face are more controlled than those of the body.

The larger muscles are easily controlled, while skin pigmentation, blinking and facial expressions are hard to control.

Nonverbal communication

What do the eyes, head and shoulders communicate?

ASSERTIVE COMMUNICATION

Free Yourself

"The eyes are the mirror of the soul".

Maintaining eye contact is a sign of respect and interest even though it can make some people feel uncomfortable.

Not looking into the eyes, so having your attention elsewhere, indicates little interest or shyness. Generally, those who avoid eye contact are perceived as insincere.

Facial mimicry is extremely rapid, lasting a fraction of a second it can be useful to emphasize an emotion by emphasizing the microexpressions and repeating them several times.

Microexpressions last about 3 seconds; if continued for a longer time, they can be interpreted as inauthentic, therefore possibly concealing a false emotion.

The position of the head, on the other hand, can convey the degree of self-confidence. Holding your head up will make you feel more confident and help get more attention by giving you more authority. Leaning the head to one side while listening is perceived as tender and sweet.

The perfect posture for excellent communication is relaxed, avoiding stiff shoulders, thus making the safety and authority of the person easily perceived.

Stiff, raised shoulders are one of the greatest indices of insecurity and anxiety.

What do the gestures of the arms and legs, and physical contact indicate?

If the arms are crossed, they can indicate tension. In more extreme cases, by closing the fists and stiffening the arms, they can communicate hostility.

Hand gestures are generally very numerous. To emphasize what you are communicating, you have to move them in a large and controlled way,

ASSERTIVE COMMUNICATION

Free Yourself

so that the movement itself seems more spontaneous. Gestures must be calm and natural, so that they support the flow of speech.

Sometimes, hand movements may not be accompanied by speech, as they communicate very clearly the states of tension, anxiety, discomfort, interest, appreciation, happiness and euphoria.

The legs, on the other hand, are the hardest part to control, especially when you are nervous, stressed or agitated.

In case of nervousness, keeping your distance from others is essential in order not to communicate a possible attack: if you exaggerate the distance, this position will result in detachment and coldness, or even insecurity.

A firm handshake or a pat on the back are part of non-verbal communication and indicate security and fidelity.

How do you improve non-verbal communication?

It starts with the elimination of unnecessary behaviors, and then training, to perceive gestures, body movements and facial expression, acquiring confidence and awareness. We need a lot of exercise and feedback from other people, in order to know the critical points and improve them in the shortest possible time.

To achieve communication goals and to ensure that messages arrive successfully, you need to be able to communicate in all aspects, not just with words. The content of the message must be conveyed with the necessary vigor, enthusiasm and dynamism in order not to risk appearing as professionals with poor communication skills.

Selling with body language

Since body language plays a fundamental role in human relationships, in sales it is even more so, since, usually, the interlocutor is not known and it is necessary to perceive his interest.

ASSERTIVE COMMUNICATION
Free Yourself

Studies indicate that non-verbal communication has a major impact in business relationships, meetings or sales sessions, as it helps the interlocutor create an immediate judgment about the seller and his sincerity.

Non-verbal communication strongly affects all aspects of life.

By reinforcing the little-controlled aspects, you will achieve very incisive and convincing communication. This can be useful in marketing, in creating one's own authority and also in uncontrolled and dangerous situations.

Knowing non-verbal communication and the meaning of gestures is the first step in learning to read the body language of others, and to control the messages you unknowingly send through your non-verbal communication.

In professional situations, if you work in sales for example, or in any context in which you have to convince someone and negotiate, knowing how to read body language and knowing how to communicate with gestures and posture are a great advantage that can prove decisive in critical moments.

Having exercises and examples of non-verbal communication allows you to train and be able to read the situation on the fly when you may be under stress and have other things to think about at the same time. In particular, with training, you will appreciate the noticeable differences between one person and another and avoid jumping to conclusions such as "if a person crosses his arms, it means he is on the defensive".

HOW TO INTERPRET THE LANGUAGE OF THE BODY

Non-verbal communication must always be interpreted in its context.

ASSERTIVE COMMUNICATION

Free Yourself

First of all, in the context of the specific person you are dealing with. Everyone has a behavioral basis that must be defined before reaching any conclusions.

For example, some people are naturally nervous, so calming gestures like finger rubbing or lip biting may not mean anything. In the case of a person who is normally calm and composed, even a small calming gesture could have an important meaning.

People cross their arms because they are defensive, because they are tired, because they are cold, because they have something on their mind that has nothing to do with you, or just because they do it out of habit.

A gesture means everything and nothing. First it must be placed in the context of the person and the situation.

PRACTICE A POSITIVE NON-VERBAL COMMUNICATION

The way we deal with others with our, often unconscious, non-verbal communication sends a specific message to the people around us. Establishing a positive message in our gestures can have a significant, albeit silent, influence on our success.

Try starting the day by setting aside 10 minutes to think about three things you are grateful for. Then, imagine three things you want to accomplish. Imagine and recall three strong emotions associated with those goals. For example, today you will have your first meeting with an important client and you want it to be a success. The emotions you want to feel and express are contentment, trust and determination.

Then, move with energy and put a genuine smile on your face. Look straight ahead with your back straight. Walk confidently, always with a smile. Your body not only communicates to others, but also to you. Emotions affect posture and posture induces emotions. If you can, with your body language, energize yourself, then it will work on others too!

ASSERTIVE COMMUNICATION

Free Yourself

EXAMPLES OF BODY GESTURES AND THEIR USE

Here are examples of non-verbal communication for exercising:

Standing position with your hands behind your back. Breathe with authority and great self-confidence. The other person's response is the kind of deference one gives to a general.

Arms raised to V. Power, confidence, and the excitement of victory. This is not a gesture that you will normally do in front of others, but it is useful for modulating your attitude and your emotions.

Open arms. Satisfaction and happiness for something good that happened. Inspire admiration and praise.

Hands on your hips. Dominance. You seem to be confident and inspire deference.

Shoulders and feet open. Confidence, dominance and being ready for action. Get people to trust your abilities.

Chest out. Dominance and strength. Inspire deference.

Upright posture. Security, strength, dominance, competence and pride. Inspire respect and confidence in your abilities.

EXERCISES TO READ THE NON-VERBAL COMMUNICATION OF OTHERS

Interpreting people's non-verbal communication is more difficult when you are emotionally involved. If, on the other hand, you observe situations in which you do not have a specific interest, you will remain more objective, which is fundamental to reading body language.

Go to a public place, a bar or a shopping center and:

Notice how a person's gender and culture affect their physical expressions.

ASSERTIVE COMMUNICATION
Free Yourself

Observe the combinations of body gestures and facial expressions. Do they match? What emotions do they express?

Go to places where you can watch two people interact with each other.

Do they mimic each other's expressions, a clear sign that they like each other?

Look for barriers and distance signs. Maybe someone moves back with his chair, or places an object between himself and the other to mean that he is hesitating and does not want to give more confidence.

Observe one person's gestures, try to understand their meaning, and then observe the other person's reaction. What are the two people communicating?

BODY LANGUAGE EXERCISES OF PEOPLE YOU KNOW

Think about 10 people you have dealt with in your job.

How would you describe their way of acting and presenting themselves? Stiff, casual, careless? Did their appearance coincide with their way of acting?

What could you have done differently with each of them to better influence their behavior? How could you introduce yourself and behave differently to influence them more?

In business meetings with coworkers, decide who is usually more candid about their emotions, and try to pick up on signs of stress.

Take quick notes on every little non-verbal communication, every little gesture, and what you think it means.

Write what a person's usual gestures are and which one's signal something specific like stress and discomfort.

ASSERTIVE COMMUNICATION

Free Yourself

Watch a comedy or television series by putting the sound on mute. Try to understand what is happening from the gestures of the characters. If gestures and facial expressions are inconsistent, either you are dealing with a bad actor, or the character is not being sincere.

THE SUB-TEXT OF VERBAL COMMUNICATION

You can use movies and television series to study the intention behind the lines of dialogue. When one person interacts with another to get an answer, they do so:

By asking a direct question.

By offering an incentive.

By leveraging emotions.

By leveraging the ego.

Helping the other person eliminate a fear.

By creating certainties or uncertainties in the mind of the other.

Using silence as a void to fill.

Notice how one person's intention produces a reaction in the other person.

Observe politicians, diplomats and others who have received training in communicating with the media.

Is the person giving direct answers or is he evasive?

When a person evades a question, what do you observe in their body language? Notice changes in their tone of voice, speech rhythm, or signs of stress.

Some people, under certain circumstances, speak without subtext, meaning they say exactly what they think. But often there is a hidden meaning beneath the surface of the words that is implicit in the consequences that the words produce.

ASSERTIVE COMMUNICATION

Free Yourself

EXERCISES ON YOUR MANAGEMENT

Look for people you trust to point out what your body language is. What are your usual gestures? How do you behave in a generic situation? Then notice how your non-verbal language changes according to your emotions.

How do you express anger? From head to toe, from the moment you are annoyed to the moment you are furious, what is your body language?

What signals do you express when you are nervous? Don't just consider gestures, but also the energy levels of your non-verbal language.

How do you change your behavior when you are on the defensive? Do you round your shoulders? Do you move behind the desk? Do you cross your arms?

The more you can be precise in analyzing your gestures, the more you will be able to control it when the time comes. We often notice our emotions, but they are still expressed by our body. By observing ourselves, we can better understand ourselves.

INTERPRETING STRESS RESPONSES IN NON-VERBAL COMMUNICATION

Stress responses are an important part of non-verbal communication. Stress does not mean just work stress, but every situation with imposes some form of discomfort.

People usually have their own way of expressing stress. You walk into an office, sit down for an important meeting, speak in front of an audience, and your body automatically relieves the stress of the situation with a series of calming gestures aimed at making you feel better.

ASSERTIVE COMMUNICATION
Free Yourself

There are those who bite their fingers, those who rub one foot against the other, those who smile, those who flip the smartphone between their fingers, etc.

Remember that every gesture is relative, its exact meaning depends on the person. Before interpreting it you need to know how that person behaves normally and, if something deviates from normal, you need to think about why. Maybe that person isn't nervous about what you said, but because he had a fight with his son that morning. Context is everything.

LISTEN

Reading the intentions of others ultimately means knowing how to listen. Do these exercises.

When you talk about a topic you know nothing about, but the other person is an expert on:

Listen and learn.

Ask questions.

Summarize what the other person said every three minutes or so to make sure you understand.

When the conversation is about a topic you know much better than the other person:

Force yourself to listen without interrupting or correcting.

In the space of three minutes, how many times would you have wanted to interrupt? How many times have you thought that that person doesn't know what they are talking about?

In these situations, it's easy to imply that the other person is saying the wrong things and not let them talk. And it is in fact likely that the other will be wrong about some things. The challenge is to wait until he has finished speaking and then understand which points need to be

ASSERTIVE COMMUNICATION
Free Yourself

addressed and how to express them in an informative rather than a critical way. Watch your non-verbal communication when you hear the other person say something wrong. What are you expressing with your attitude? Curiosity? Nuisance? Impatience?

NON-VERBAL COMMUNICATION, GESTURES AND MEANING

Non-verbal communication has a varied and subtle vocabulary that can be divided into various categories of meaning:

Gestures that serve to highlight the words, to underline their importance. For example, pointing a finger.

Gestures that serve to explain something. They add further meaning to the words or give them a more precise nuance. For example, indicating the size of something with your hands.

Gestures that serve to release stress and discomfort. Like fiddling with an earring or biting your nails.

Gestures that serve to create a barrier to protect oneself, or express distance. From crossing your arms to physically placing an object in front of you.

Notice when you observe people in your daily life. Always ask yourself: What is this person really saying? What is the intention that you may not even be aware of?

You will also notice almost imperceptible microgestures on a conscious level. They are small expressions of the eyes, small tensions, looks that appear for just milliseconds. They are none other than thoughts which for an instant make their appearance in the physical world of the body.

ASSERTIVE COMMUNICATION

Free Yourself

CHAPTER 12 NLP

Often in the company we hear about NLP: there are those who present it as the magic wand that transforms our life into a world of success.

The truth is, they are selling you something, and NLP can do it very well. But underneath there is much more: let's discover it in a journey that began in the early 70s.

What would later become NLP began in the early 1970s with Richard Bandler, a graduate student at the University of California in Santa Cruz, where he was majoring in mathematics and computer science. Studying behavioral science he found himself having to transcribe and edit videotapes relating to seminars conducted by Fritz Perls, a famous Gestalt psychotherapist. Watching and re-watching these films several times, Bandler, as if by osmosis, began to understand how to lead therapeutic groups as effectively as those of Perls.

He began to wonder how he had done it: it was quite easy, given his background in mathematics and computer science, to ask the question in terms of behavioral "equations" that did not always produce the same "answers". Meanwhile, at the same university, a certain John Grinder - at the time assistant professor of linguistics and specialist in Noam Chomsky's Transformational Grammar - was conducting similar studies on the processes that lead people to "absorb" and adopt the behaviors of others.

Grinder thus proposed to Bandler to apply these principles to the understanding of how a therapeutic process works. "Teach me what you can do, and I'll teach you how you do it," Grinder told Bandler. Thus took shape the central process of NLP: the so-called Modeling.

Bandler and Grinder spent the next period immersing themselves in an impressive series of "exemplary" performances taken by anyone who was excellent in every human field: therapists, public speakers,

ASSERTIVE COMMUNICATION

Free Yourself

sportsmen, communicators, artists, other successful men and women. After observing and recording them, the next step was to break down all the elements of their behavior, bit by bit, to evaluate how each contributed to the final outcome. Through this sifting process, they finally came to obtain a coded model of the significant structures of a given exemplary behavior.

It is made up of external actions, ie behaviors, linked to specific abilities, but also and above all, internal: expectations, beliefs, values, first of all; and rapid passages of visual, auditory, bodily and emotional elements, which, if not extrapolated, often remain unconscious. Their mix, which is unique, results in excellence in that specific skill. All this is extractable through direct observation and interviews, because all human experience is linguistically codable. And as such it is also transmissible. With this method Bandler and Grinder were able to observe who was excellent at something, translate his excellence into concrete and precise sequences, describe them linguistically and at that point make them their own, becoming themselves excellent in those skills: they became "magicians", in fact, and from there was born one of their first writings, "The structure of Magic".

Not wizards of sales, or of motivation, but wizards in knowing how to learn - and teach - any skill, because they know how to grasp its invisible structure. Here, then, is a first definition of NLP: Neuro Linguistic Programming studies the structure of subjective experience.

NLP is often understood as a synonym for communication, indeed, good communication. Which then some make veer into tangent concepts, such as persuasion and manipulation, but this is a different kettle of fish that we will discuss later. NLP is actually also good communication, addressed both to others and to oneself.

There are a lot of rules and techniques to create it, but no one dwells on another, much more important, dimension: it comes from a "mentality", from an anti-intuitive way of thinking with respect to our cognitive and emotional "habits". Here are the first steps to start getting into it.

ASSERTIVE COMMUNICATION

Free Yourself

"The map is not the territory"

We are not passive receivers of stimuli that come to us from the outside: we live in a reality that we ourselves construct moment by moment, perceiving it, interpreting it, sharing it, according to our "internal" world. This is why reality does not exist in itself, but it is an experience that everyone has, very personal. The problem is that we forget this, believing that our reality is the objective one: this is where misunderstandings and conflicts arise.

A trivial example: if ten people go to visit the same new city, ask each of them to tell you in exactly two minutes what that city is like. Everyone will tell you different things, sometimes even antithetical, because everyone is struck by different things that depend on tastes, emotions, personal experiences and - here's the point - different mental assets.

Our feeling good or bad with respect to an event does not arise from the event itself, but from the meaning we give it according to our internal maps. "She did not reply to my message, it means that she is angry", or "She did not invite me to the meeting, she has no respect for me", are classic examples of how we build a reality that is not based on "objective" data but on our purely internal beliefs, perceptions, emotions, and expectations. To stop it, we must remember the ideas that we are dealing with are hypotheses, which must be verified.

"You did not understand!" "I know what you have to do!"

We often confuse our world map with reality, as we have seen before. This has a direct impact on how we communicate with other people, because we tend to interpret and judge what they tell us with our own parameters.

The golden rule of NLP - which then applies to Counseling and Coaching - is: listen as if you were naked, stripping yourself as much as possible from your preconceptions, with a healthy sense of curiosity. And take responsibility for what you communicate by really listening to the feedback that comes to you from the other person. His response will tell you if what you intended to communicate was truly understood, or

ASSERTIVE COMMUNICATION

Free Yourself

misunderstood. It is not that you "misunderstood", but it is I who have explained myself in a way that is not effective for you.

Let's get to the heart of the matter: some practical applications of NLP

After introducing what NLP is, where and how it started, and what mentality it develops, here are some applications, to begin to understand concretely how it works. Today's journey begins with a... green duck.

Don't think of a green duck, don't think of a green duck, don't think of it!

But...the green duck peeps out, appears, and then stands there in front of you and doesn't want to leave. You try to chase it away, pushing it away, putting a cross on it, making it disappear behind a curtain, looking for the switch to turn off the light, but to no avail. What if instead of the duck there was a jar of Nutella and you were on a diet? Or a cigarette and you wanted to quit smoking? Or a co-worker you feel like scolding? You would have your "object" of desire in front of you that, with all its might, reminds you how good it is, there is no diet or prescription that works.

This is a tiny example of how our brain works: in this case it tells us that it cannot process negatives. We project the example to simple attitudes that we put in place on a daily basis: from the prohibitions we give to our children, to the problems that arise at work, to performance in sport and music, to the goals we set ourselves, we tend damnably to emphasize what we don't want, and - coincidentally - we struggle to get out.

The solution that NLP offers us lies precisely in the green duck: thinking about hunting it always brings us back to it, thinking about the problem predisposes us to think with the logic of the problem itself. It's like when

ASSERTIVE COMMUNICATION
Free Yourself

we say "I don't have to get upset when I speak in public": we are commanding our brain to think about the problem and we are activating it to produce anxiety. The green duck cannot be eliminated - this is the classic old problem-solving approach - but it must be dissolved, replaced with something else we want to achieve in its place.

To begin with, the first question to ask is: if I don't want the green duck anymore, what do I want instead? And so: by quitting smoking, depriving myself of Nutella, or not being agitated when I speak in public, what do I get out of it that is important to me? Thus, I begin to bring out positive results and values that define why it is important for me to achieve those results. Not only that: I am configuring my internal operating system to imagine myself as if I had already reached them, and the system adapts, making the work attractive and the resources necessary to achieve it more available. In other words, motivation arises.

This work is done in NLP with some very precise tools.

To begin with, the Metamodel is used, a set of linguistic questions that refers to the maieutic approach to enter the "deep map" and discover useful information for change: the effect that is usually obtained is that the person discovers what he really wants, why he can't change, what beliefs bind him to always repeating the same unsatisfactory behaviors. Sometimes this path may be enough to unlock things, or you need to continue.

Next to the Metamodel, Logical Levels are used, a series of scalar questions that make it possible to clarify expectations, purposes, values, even reaching identity and mission. By doing so, any "internal saboteurs" are immediately highlighted and their motivations are enhanced, which at that point become the fuel to reach the goal.

Once the ground has been prepared, one can work with the so-called "VAK Submodalities", coding the way in which the brain creates a representation of the desired state. Think about it: think about the exact moment when you have reached your goal and close your eyes, what do you see? An image or a film? Are you inside yourself or do you see

ASSERTIVE COMMUNICATION
Free Yourself

yourself from the outside? Is it in color, or black and white? Are there any sounds? How loud are they? What do they say? Where do they come from? Do you feel an emotion somewhere in your body? What happens if you move it? And finally, put yourself in the most suitable and congruent posture with the result: how does your perception change? It is possible to manipulate these sub-modalities in order to amplify their effect and make it even more attractive and motivating, dissolving any sources of negativity. The change is permanent, because our brain adapts immediately to whatever makes it feel better.

And finally, here is the road map to reach the goal: the object is defined, which must be under one's own responsibility and measurable, it is divided into small sub-objectives that serve to create positive feedback and get us used to success. The resources are identified, and finally the temporal dimension is safeguarded. What is all this called? We can call it NLP, we can call it Goal Setting, or Coaching. There are many names, what matters to us is that we have begun to experiment how to manage our cognitive schemes more effectively to obtain concrete improvements in our life.

ASSERTIVE COMMUNICATION
Free Yourself

CHAPTER 13 NLP TECHNIQUES

Neuro Linguistic Programming (NLP) is a kind of "manual for the brain". In fact, NLP techniques can be very effective in changing the way you experience the world by transforming your thoughts and emotions on reality, to achieve a more balanced and beneficial state of mind. Learning NLP techniques will allow you to effectively manage your emotions and change negative thought patterns that harm you or limit your development. It's like "accessing" the brain and changing its programming.

NLP attempts to understand how people organize their thoughts, feelings, language and behavior, providing them with a model for achieving the results they propose in different areas of life.

According to NLP, we all have unique mind maps that are the result of how we perceive and filter information through the senses. In NLP the basic mind map is called "first access" and is made up of internal images, sounds, tactile awareness, internal sensations, tastes and smells, as it is created primarily through the senses.

Later we assign personal meaning to the stimuli we receive from the outside world. Thus, we form a second mental map in which we assign words to internal images, sounds and feelings, tastes and smells. It is our linguistic map.

Our behavior is the response to both maps and the result of them. This means that we do not simply react to what happens around us, but react according to the meaning we attribute to the facts, which depends on many psychological factors, from our past experiences to our expectations or our state of mind.

NLP techniques allow us to work internally on this linguistic map, to change our behavior and the emotions generated by situations.

ASSERTIVE COMMUNICATION

Free Yourself

Effective NLP techniques to feel better and achieve balance

1. Dissociation

Have you ever found yourself in a situation that made you feel bad? Maybe something has made you nervous or depressed, a pattern that repeats itself in some situations. In these cases, when such feelings seem to be automatic, and are triggered when certain circumstances converge, the NLP technique called dissociation can be very useful.

Start by identifying the emotion you feel, it can be fear, anger, discomfort or sadness. So, imagine being able to step out of your body and look at yourself from the outside, looking at the situation from the perspective of an outside observer. Notice how that emotion changes dramatically.

This technique is even more powerful if, after imagining that you have left your body, you go back to imagining that you have also left your new body and look at it from another perspective. It is a double dissociation that will allow you to establish a huge psychological distance from what is happening and better manage the emotions you are experiencing.

2. Re-contextualize the situation

When you are immersed in a negative situation where you feel helpless because you cannot change it, this technique will become your best ally. It is about re-contextualizing the negative situation in order to experience it in a more positive way.

Imagine, for example, that your relationship is over. It may seem terrible to you at first, but you can recontextualize it. What are the benefits of being single? It's about giving new meaning to the breakup and not just focusing on the negative aspects.

It is normal for us to feel panicked or discouraged in certain situations, but this only generates more difficulties, especially when you don't have control over what's happening. The best way to clear your mind and make more rational decisions is to have a more complete view, which implies the possibility of seeing the positive as well.

3. Anchoring

Anchoring is one of the most used NLP techniques and also one of the most effective. It is about creating an association between a stimulus and a response through "anchors". It is very useful when you have to deal with stressful situations or situations that generate negative emotions.

It is about choosing the emotion you want to feel, such as trust, happiness, calm ... and anchoring it to your body through a simple movement, such as pressing a fingernail, pulling your earlobe or touching the knuckle of a finger.

You must start by recalling the memory of a situation in which you felt safe, strong, happy or calm (the emotion you wish to anchor). Recreate the memory with all the details. As you relive that feeling, touch the part of your body where you will create the anchor. You have to repeat the exercise several times, always remembering the different situations that generated the feeling you want to anchor.

With practice, when you find yourself in a situation that makes you feel bad, it will be enough for you to perform that simple movement to activate the emotion you have associated it with. It is a very effective and powerful technique, although it requires constant work to achieve the anchor. The more you practice, the stronger the emotional response you activate.

4. Swish

This NLP technique is very effective in reducing or even eliminating the power of recurring negative thoughts, or subtracting emotional impact from both past events whose affects you continue to carry or future

ASSERTIVE COMMUNICATION

Free Yourself

events that generate fear or anxiety. With this technique you will not have to fight against those thoughts or emotions, but simply train your mind to respond differently to generate a new thought or emotion.

First of all, you need to identify the unwanted thought (activator) and the feeling it evokes. It also determines what the trigger is, such as the image or situation that triggers that negative thought. So, you have to choose a replacement thought. What would you like to think and feel instead of getting stuck in negative thinking?

You also need to make sure that the unwanted thought does not require you to take any action, it is not a problem to be solved, but simply an annoying idea generated by an irrational belief.

So you need to focus on creating a replacement image. Recreate it down to the smallest detail. This way you will not fight the thought or the emotion, but you will simply replace it.

5. Emotional record

This NLP technique, which is actually a visualization exercise, is very useful for getting rid of the emotions that negatively affect us; the ones that, no matter how hard we try, will not leave us, from sadness to anger or disappointment.

Choose one of the negative feelings that bother you. The ideal would be to start with a not very intense sensation. As you practice, you can start working with stronger emotions.

Focus on determining in which part of your body you feel this sensation. Note the end points and the direction of the feeling. Suppose the sensation begins at point A and ends at point B.

Now imagine that, as the sensation moves from A to B, at B it leaves your body and re-enters through point A, forming a complete circle. Observe the speed with which the disc rotates as it forms and imagine the color it has.

ASSERTIVE COMMUNICATION
Free Yourself

Next, visualize a hole in the center of the disc and place an imaginary lever in the middle, squeeze the lever with your hands. Move that lever so that the disc / sensation rotates faster and faster. You can mentally count to three and push the lever forward, pulling the disc out of the body.

Keep holding it in front of you. Look at the circle, its speed and color. Now replace that color with a more beautiful one. Rotate the lever very quickly so that the end of the right hand goes to the left hand and vice versa. Now look at the disc. You will notice that the direction in which it moves has reversed.

Now mentally count to three and forcefully pull the puck towards your body. You will immediately notice a feeling of relief.

ASSERTIVE COMMUNICATION

Free Yourself

CHAPTER 14 ASSERTIVENESS TECHNIQUES FOR SUCCESS AT WORK

Self-esteem and assertiveness are two factors at the service of individual well-being and success: in the workplace they are integrated within the concept of organizational well-being.

When we feel good at work, we are more productive, more likely to communicate and interact positively and, above all, more motivated to learn and improve in order to achieve higher and higher goals.

Work well-being is a broad topic, which should be treated from different points of view: what we will focus on today is your point of view, that of the worker. Understanding why it is important to feel good, physically and mentally, at work will take us through the concept of self-confidence and assertiveness, two fundamental factors to be truly happy at work, to conclude with practical advice to help you be more assertive and have more confidence in yourself.

Assertiveness derives from the word "assert" (assert, affirm oneself) which outlines the human attitude to express one's opinions and ideas, to defend one's rights, to communicate one's emotions, without fear or imposing oneself on others. US psychologists Emmons and Smith defined this concept just as:

"A behavior that allows a person to act in his own interest, to defend his point of view without exaggerated anxiety, to express his feelings with sincerity and ease and to defend his rights without ignoring those of others".

Assertiveness is an attitude to be kept in balance: at the right level it will lead us to more easily reach our work goals, to create a healthy and stimulating environment around us and to minimize tensions and

ASSERTIVE COMMUNICATION
Free Yourself

conflicts; all this always showing education, sensitivity and listening towards those who relate to us.

Being too assertive could make us, in the eyes of others, an arrogant person or even a bully, who wants to impose his will on others, without considering their opinions and needs. On the other hand, a too low level of assertiveness characterizes a basically passive personality, who is unable to express his ideas and appears submissive in various circumstances for fear of the judgment of others.

Assertiveness at work leads us to be more responsible and empathetic, to survive even complicated situations with serenity, to improve our relationships with employers and colleagues, to solve problems with safety and proactivity, improving the company climate and well-being among colleagues.

After understanding the benefits of this approach, let's move on to practice. Good news: assertiveness is born ... or made! This characteristic is partly innate, but it can certainly be trained and stimulated every day with small exercises that over time can become a great strength.

USEFUL TIPS TO BE CONFIDENT WITHOUT EVER BEING ARROGANT

1. **Don't put off what you could do today, until tomorrow**

We often tend to postpone the start of projects, new activities that we have in mind for a long time or tasks that we find particularly difficult or beyond our reach. What blocks us is not so much the lack of time or capacity, it is the fear of discovering we are not able to complete the task, or facing a possible failure and, above all, the judgment of others.

Accept the challenges, get out of your comfort zone, face your fears step by step and start that activity today that you keep putting off. The next time, you will have less fear and, gradually, you will feel more and more

ASSERTIVE COMMUNICATION

Free Yourself

confident in yourself and will be able to face increasingly challenging situations.

Becoming assertive is a journey, not an instant decision or an overnight change.

2. Accept compliments without embarrassment

Those who do not feel sure of themselves or do not believe in their abilities, often find it difficult to accept compliments, replying "It is not true", or "I have not done anything special", to the point of sometimes perceiving them as mockery. A compliment must be accepted without embarrassment, a nice smiling "thank you" is an excellent response. Your successes are deserved... and they should also be rightly celebrated!

3. Learn to say NO

Being assertive does not mean saying yes in all circumstances, quite the contrary. Learning to say no is essential to protect ourselves, overcoming the fear of disappointing those who work with us and the risk of becoming prey to bullying people. If you do not consider any request from colleagues or superiors to be objective or useful, you have the right to respond negatively, always politely, and calmly explaining your reasons.

4. Assert your opinions without overpowering others

You will often discuss things with colleagues: if you want to assert your idea, explain it passionately but politely, but also be ready to accept that your proposals may not be chosen or shared. If it's not, ask why, to understand, and don't insist with arrogance.

When faced with a problem, try not to focus so much on the causes but on possible solutions. Breathing control in these cases can help to

ASSERTIVE COMMUNICATION

Free Yourself

maintain calm and the right tone of conversation: in balance between the controversial person who loses his temper and the immobility of those who are unable to react, problem solving skills lie in the middle.

Another useful skill in these situations is negotiation, characteristic of a person who wants to assert his ideas and opinions, because he considers them valid, without diminishing or overwhelming those of others.

5. Check your body

When talking to a colleague or supervisor, remember to maintain eye contact, a body posture that is erect and not bent, a tone of voice that is neither too high nor too low and the right distance between you and your interlocutor. Remember that the management of your body and the expressiveness of your face speak to both you and those in front of you: you will feel more confident in yourself and you will be able to be more assertive and others will perceive you in the same way.

6. Admit your mistakes and apologize when it is okay to do so

A typical behavior of a person with a passive attitude is to constantly apologize, even when there is no need.

"Sorry if I disturbed you", "Sorry if I'm stealing your time", "Sorry to bother you", "Maybe what I said is wrong, but ..." An assertive person transforms apologies into thanks and positive forms of communication: "Thanks for your availability", "Thanks for waiting", "I have a request for you that will surely help me".

Rather, an apology is necessary when we realize that we have made a mistake or have engaged in negative behavior, which has hurt or harmed someone. Everyone makes mistakes. The difference lies in the ability to admit their mistakes with humility and to offer to make up for it.

ASSERTIVE COMMUNICATION
Free Yourself

7. Don't be afraid to ask for clarification, help and advice

A phrase to keep in mind, almost like a mantra, as we ask ourselves whether asking that question is "the worst thing that can happen is receiving a no". The ability to ask for help when facing a difficult moment, and to seek advice and other points of view when in doubt, is not a sign of weakness, quite the contrary!

Comparison with others helps us grow and make the best decisions: sometimes we feel as if we are clouded with fear ... but in most cases, doubts are resolved just by expressing them aloud. These behaviors are characteristic of mature people who know their limits, but who show the will to overcome them even with the help of others.

You will see that by keeping in mind and applying these tips, day after day, you will feel more confident, you will be able to manage your time at work better (leaving behind you the unpleasant feeling of always being out of your depth). You will get better personal results and, above all, you will feel less anxiety and stress.

We know it's not easy to keep all these things in mind: choose a point to improve on and start with that! Step by step it will come naturally to you.

ASSERTIVE COMMUNICATION

Free Yourself

CHAPTER 15 HOW TO BE ASSERTIVE IN LIFE AS A COUPLE

How important is it, in the couple, to say no, to affirm your needs and feelings?

It is really important, because otherwise you risk living the relationship with the idea of making the other happy and never disappointing him; and in order not to be left behind, you risk becoming monotonous, obvious, boring, or worse: dissatisfied and unhappy.

With assertiveness we refer to a term that presupposes the ability of people to affirm their opinion with conviction. No, don't think about aggressive, arrogant or manipulative people. Indeed, assertiveness presupposes the ability to affirm one's opinions without fear, but with respect for the other, accepting criticism and coming into contact with emotions.

Therefore, it also concerns the great ability to know how to say no, to situations in which you are not happy, to things you do not want to do, to moments of sexuality that you do not want to share.

As a couple, in friendship, in the family, at work, affirming yourself respecting the other is fundamental, since communicating well what you want, avoiding that habit of thinking "the other will understand me, he must understand me because he knows me well", allows the person before us to understand exactly what we are asking for, what we lack or what makes us feel bad, and positively orientates a faster and more concrete response to the satisfaction of both.

Communication is the main basis for maintaining a lasting relationship and for overcoming the crises that inevitably go through it. A good assertive style of communication allows the couple not to lead to

ASSERTIVE COMMUNICATION

Free Yourself

dissatisfaction and manipulative or passive mechanisms. To understand better, we often fall into the trap of "I do what he wants so he won't leave me, I will seem less burdensome, more available", or simply to make the other happy.

It is necessary not to forget what makes you feel good, because if we expect the other to understand what troubles us and take action to solve it, the basis is to understand what you really want and then communicate it with certainty to the partner to avoid confusion.

In fact, communication is one of the elements that determine the success of a loving relationship.

So, it is necessary to express what you do not want and, in case, with kindness, explain the reasons, starting from how you feel and what makes you feel bad, not accusing the other of some lack and not diminishing him compared to others. So, saying no to sex that we don't want at that moment, to a kiss that you don't feel like giving, to a trip or a dinner with relatives and friends, etc., is not rude, it is respect for yourself. it's good. Say no, because you just don't feel like it!

To understand what we really feel and communicate it to the other, let's stop every now and then, listen to our body, which often sends us messages that we do not understand. Stop and ask yourself, "How am I, how am I in this thing?" A real listening, without judgment or thoughts, simply listening to how you would be in a situation.

It is important not to lose sight of what we really want and feel. So, stop and breathe! Now, together, stop and breathe. Starting with three deep breaths where you let the breath go even in a noisy way, then get ready to close your eyes.

Have you closed them? Good! (Maybe first read this; reading with your eyes closed is difficult!). Find a comfortable position, sitting or lying down, close your eyes and just breathe! It is the most natural thing in the world! In fact, you don't have to force your breath or judge whether it is too fast, slow, heavy or whatever, just observe it, as if you are looking at it from the outside.

ASSERTIVE COMMUNICATION

Free Yourself

Once you have found a comfortable position, start listening to your breathing. Let it go freely, effortlessly, just listen to it. Breathe in and out and every two or three breaths, observe the texture of the air, where your breath comes in, how you feel it, if it is cool or warm, where you breathe from. You just have to observe, there is no right or wrong way to do it.

You reconnect with your body and after a while, continuing to inhale and exhale, ask yourself: "How am I now? Is something bothering me? Is there something I would like to change? Or that I would not like to do?" and listen to yourself.

Before communicating anything, it is important to understand what our goals and priorities are.

Being aware of these two aspects allows us to make our requests or express our point of view in a clear and concise way.

Being assertive is part of the win-win logic in which two people undertake to find an agreement between two opposing desires to reach a compromise that satisfies them both.

There are five "golden rules" to start communicating assertively.

1. **We listen to each other actively**

When a person is giving us an opinion, we must try to listen to it without prejudice, in order to understand his point of view.

We may find some strategies useful:

- Reformulation or repeating what we are told to see if we understood: "If I understand correctly, you are telling me that ..."

ASSERTIVE COMMUNICATION

Free Yourself

- Formulation of questions on aspects that are not clear to us with phrases such as "If I understand correctly you would like ..."
- Summary at the end of the speech in order to highlight the most important points and give feedback on the fact that we have actively listened.

2. We speak in the first person

When we use the first person, others can easily understand that we are expressing a need.

We can use some phrases such as: "I would like this work to be completed by Friday"; "I think the work you have done is good but I would like that ..."

When we have a different opinion from others we try to replace "You are wrong" with "I disagree" so that people understand that we are not expressing a judgment about them but that, while we appreciate them, we have a different opinion about a certain topic.

3. 3.We express our needs clearly and concisely

To facilitate others understanding us, we try to express them in a concrete way by referring to real facts.

The phrase: "I wish you were more careful in your work" can confuse your interlocutor and lead him to ask himself some questions such as: What are you referring to? What part of the job?

He could be put on the defensive because he receives a judgment about his person and not about the behavior.

We could assertively restructure the sentence into some passages.

- Behavior description: "You have been late submitting your work for about a month and the last three reports you gave me contained some grammatical errors."

ASSERTIVE COMMUNICATION

Free Yourself

- Expression of emotions and positive evaluation of the person: "I am very worried about you because I know that you are a precise person".
- Expression of need: "I would like to be able to talk about it with you to understand how we can deal with this situation, since I need the work, I have assigned to you to be done in a precise way in order to be able to present it to the client".
- Proposal: "What do you say we talk about it this afternoon?"

4. We communicate our NOs effectively

There are some situations in which we are asked for our contribution in work or our private life that creates difficulties for us, because it would add up to busy days, full of commitments.

How can I say no?

First of all, let us realize the consequences of our no, in order to have a clear vision of events.

When we refuse the proposal, we always accompany the no with a very specific reason.

An example could be: "I can't stay longer than working hours because I've already made a commitment for tonight".

When it is very difficult for us to express a no, in addition to the motivation, we can accompany our refusal with an alternative proposal:

"I can't stay longer than working hours because I have a commitment. How about if we look at the document together tomorrow morning?"

5. Pay attention to non-verbal language

Assertiveness is also expressed through our body language.

ASSERTIVE COMMUNICATION

Free Yourself

Some strategies that can be useful to us concern maintaining eye contact with our interlocutor, an open stance, an alert facial expression and a firm tone of voice, dwelling on the keywords.

Knowing how to communicate assertively is an art we can learn!

We begin to train our assertiveness by experimenting in situations that seem easier to manage, and in small steps, we will be able to deal with situations that now seem really thorny.

Assertiveness is a balanced type of communication, and requires you to be forthright about your own wants and needs, while still considering the rights, needs and wants of others. Aggressive behavior, on the other hand, is based on prevarication. When you are aggressive, the power you use is selfish: taking what you want, often without asking.

In everyday situations it is not easy to be assertive.

Suppose, for example, you disagree with your boss. In a situation of this type we can implement three types of behavior:

1) Stay passive, hurt, without saying anything. This triggers anger, creates resentment, and undermines your self-esteem and health. You behave passively when you accept what others say and how they behave, while within you there is disagreement. With this behavior you allow people to control your life. Generally, those who choose this behavior want to avoid disagreements and conflicts. You don't express your opinions each time, for fear of not being accepted or understood.

2) You become aggressive and show your anger and dissatisfaction out loud. However, this behavior only negatively affects your relationship with your boss and you may even get fired.

3) Act assertively and communicate to your boss, fearlessly, how you feel when you disagree with him and when you are angry about

ASSERTIVE COMMUNICATION
Free Yourself

something he said or did. You can to do this diplomatically, and with kindness and are able to suggest a balanced and reasonable way to resolve the matter.

As you can see, the third option is the best.

When there is assertiveness, there is no fear of expressing your disagreement.

There are various ways to develop assertiveness. Being assertive can be difficult at first, especially for people who are usually passive or who are always trying to please others and avoid expressing their opinions... but this doesn't have to be a reason to give up.

Obviously, I recommend that you start with small matters, for example, asking for a better table at the restaurant, requesting to have a cup of hot coffee, pointing out that yours is lukewarm, asking someone to call you later if you are busy.

Remember that being assertive means knowing how to express your opinions and thoughts - no one knows what you want unless you tell them.

What matters is to express yourself calmly and respectfully.

Also remember to express your thoughts and ask for something without apologizing or giving excuses: if you apologize too much, especially when it is not necessary, you weaken your assertiveness and show weakness.

One of the main benefits of being assertive is that it can help you become more confident.

In general, assertive people:

Get things done by treating people with fairness and respect and are treated by others equally in return.

ASSERTIVE COMMUNICATION
Free Yourself

Recognize each other's worth and can quickly find common ground.

They are good problem solvers and feel capable of doing whatever it takes to find the best solution to the problems they encounter.

Are less anxious and stressed, they are self-confident, and they don't feel threatened or victimized when things don't go as planned or as expected.

If you would like to be a person with the characteristics I have just described, read below which techniques to use to develop and increase your assertiveness.

1. Value yourself and your rights. To be more assertive, you need to gain a good understanding of yourself, as well as a strong belief in your intrinsic worth. This self-awareness is the basis of self-confidence and assertive behavior: it will help you recognize that you deserve to be treated with dignity and respect, give you the confidence to defend your rights and protect them, remaining true to yourself, to your desires, and your needs. It is vital to make sure that it does not develop into a blind sense of selfishness. Remember that your rights, thoughts, feelings, needs and wants are as important as everyone's, but no more important than anyone else's.

2. Express your needs and wishes with confidence. If you are going to express your full potential, then you need to make sure that your priorities, needs and desires are met. Don't wait for someone else to recognize what you need - you could wait forever! Take the initiative and start identifying the things you want. Then, set goals so you can achieve them. Once you've done this, you can tell your boss or colleague exactly what you need to help you achieve these goals clearly and confidently. If what you want is not possible right now, ask (politely) that your request not be abandoned but re-evaluated in a few months: find ways to make requests that avoid sacrificing the needs of others.

ASSERTIVE COMMUNICATION
Free Yourself

3. Recognize that you cannot control the behavior of others. Don't make the mistake of accepting responsibility for how people react to your assertiveness. If, for example, they become angry or resentful towards you, try to avoid reacting in the same way. Remember that you can control yourself and your behavior, so do your best to remain calm and measured if things get heavy. As long as you are respectful and don't violate someone else's needs, then you have the right to say or do whatever you want.

4. Express yourself positively. It is important to say what you have in mind, even when you have a difficult problem to deal with, but you need to do it constructively. Don't be afraid to stand up for yourself and confront people who challenge you and / or your rights. You can even afford to be angry! But remember to control your emotions and always be respectful.

5. Be open to criticism and compliments. Accept both positive and negative feedback. If you disagree with the criticism you receive, you need to be ready to say it, but not be aggressive.

6. Learn to say "No". Saying "No" is hard to do, especially when you're not used to it, but it's essential if you want to become more assertive. Knowing your limitations and the work you are able to do will help you manage your businesses more effectively and identify areas of your work that make you feel better or worse. Remember that you absolutely cannot do everything or please everyone, so it is important to protect your time and workload by saying "no" when necessary.

7. Use assertive communication techniques. - Use "I want", "I need" or "I feel" to convey your point of view in a decisive way. For example, "I

ASSERTIVE COMMUNICATION
Free Yourself

strongly believe that we need to involve a third party to mediate this disagreement."

8. Don't forget about empathy. Always try to recognize and understand how the other person views the situation; then, after considering their point of view, express what you need from her. For example, "I understand that you have problems working with Irene but this project must be completed by Friday. Let's all sit down and come up with a plan together".

9. Don't be afraid to ask for more time. Be honest and tell the person that you need a few minutes to compose your thoughts. For example, you might say "your request caught me off guard. I'll get back to you within half an hour".

Being assertive means having a strong sense of yourself and your worth and recognizing that you deserve to get what you want.

ASSERTIVE COMMUNICATION
Free Yourself

CONCLUSIONS

Assertiveness is a fundamental skill for having good relationships. It allows us to express ourselves, our needs, our ideas, opinions, without, however, overpowering others. Assertive behavior allows us to adopt an appropriate relational style based on the context, to give importance to ourselves by recognizing the importance of the opinions and needs of the other. A sort of: "I am important but you are too", "My emotions and my opinions have a value like yours".

Assertive behavior presupposes:

- A frank expression of one's needs, desires, emotions.
- Appropriate actions in order to get what the person wants.
- Respect for the rights of others.
- Absence of feelings of guilt, embarrassment or anger as the expression of one's needs is adequate and consistent.
- Good self-esteem.

EXERCISE:

After identifying your relationship style, try to recall an episode in which you behaved passively or aggressively. Try to remember all aspects of the situation well, as if you are reliving them right now.

- What were your thoughts at that time?
- What emotions did you feel?
- How did you behave?
- At what exact moment did you implement that behavior?
- After some time, do you think there could have been a more adequate way to behave in that situation?

ASSERTIVE COMMUNICATION
Free Yourself

Then, think of an episode in which you engaged in assertive behavior.

- What happened in that situation? Where were you? With whom?
- What were your thoughts at that time?
- How did you feel?
- How did you behave?
- Do you think your behavior was appropriate to the situation?

If the answer is yes, what allowed you to implement it?

Now try to reflect on what you notice different between these two events ...

How do your thoughts, emotions, behaviors differ?

To be assertive it is first necessary to change all the thoughts I formulate, all the opinions and beliefs I have towards myself.

There are often beliefs such as:

1) **I absolutely must get approval and affection from all people relevant to me.**

The truth is that:

- I cannot please everyone.
- As I like some people more than others, the same happens to others towards me.
- If someone does not like me, this does not mean that I am not a lovable person and worthy of affection / love.
- Approval and affection must be built over time, we cannot expect them a priori.
- Is the other really rejecting me, or am I interpreting the situation because of my fear and my uncovered painful theme?

ASSERTIVE COMMUNICATION
Free Yourself

- Approval is not an absolute concept, I can be approved for some aspects of myself but not for everything, as I can do towards the other.

Think about a person you know, who is damn unpleasant to you but nice to others, it can happen, right? We all happen to have people we get along well with, and others we don't get along with. It is incredibly subjective!

2) I must always be capable and up to the situation, I can't make mistakes.

I have to consider that:

- Nobody is perfect and we all make mistakes. No individual existing on earth is capable of being always competent and up to any situation.
- Errors and mistakes are part of human nature.
- If I do make a mistake, it's not the end of the world.
- Not all errors have the same weight and I can try to think differently based on their "severity".

3) If a person behaves badly or differently from what I would do, he is bad and I have to make him pay for it.

It is useful to change perspective:

- It's true he hurt me, but that doesn't mean he's a bad person.
- I can't know if he intentionally wanted to hurt me just to have this effect on me.
- I cannot impose my standards of judgment and behavior on others.
- If a person behaved badly with me, it is necessary that I defend myself, but it is not useful for me to feel so bad.

ASSERTIVE COMMUNICATION

Free Yourself

Try to:

Explain to the other your point of view, why you did not like his behavior. Defend yourself if necessary, but do not try to impose your vision of reality on the other.

4) It's terrible that things don't go as I say!

Ok ...

- This time it went badly, I didn't want it to go like this, but it did, I can tolerate it.
- Often things don't go our way and it doesn't just happen to us. It is not a matter of "bad luck", it just happens because for most things we are not in control.
- It is useless to get angry if it has already happened. Invest your energies in achievable goals.
- It feels bad, but I can use these energies to find new solutions.

Try to:

Think about all the times it went wrong and you finally managed to endure it, finding alternatives to resolve the situation.

Use all the energy you invest in anger and frustration to find new solutions and set new goals.

5) I feel fragile / weak, alone I cannot do it.

It happens to everyone:

- Feeling frail and weak, but that does not mean that they are unable to cope.
- We are all interdependent, this does not mean being fragile.
- How can I be sure I won't make it alone if I don't try?
- The results I get do not indicate my worth.

Try to:

ASSERTIVE COMMUNICATION

Free Yourself

Think about all those situations, even small ones, in which you managed to assert yourself.

Try it, go for it... you have nothing to lose.

> **6) I have to be careful not to hurt the other, otherwise I would be bad and selfish.**

Reflect:

- If I express a need I am not selfish, but listening to myself and loving myself.
- I am not responsible for how the other person may feel, but for how I behave.
- If I listen to my needs, I am more able to be comfortable with others, without frustration.

Try to:

Observe how you feel when you do not express your needs but indulge the other, not listening to yourself. The anger and frustration you feel later on are probably not helping you.

In order to be truly selfless and attentive to the other, I must first experience a healthy selfishness by taking care of myself and my needs. Only if I do this can I also dedicate myself to the other in a healthy way.

Main features of assertive communication

- Formulate sentences in the first person. If I describe what I feel and think about a given situation it is necessary that I do it speaking in the first person ("I believe, in my opinion, I believe that, I would like, I would like, I felt .."). I take responsibility for my thoughts, emotions, behaviors. This means that if the other has made me angry about something I will not say "you did this wrong ..." rather "I am very angry about what you did .."

ASSERTIVE COMMUNICATION
Free Yourself

- Recognize the mental state of the other. For example, if the other asks me for a favor that I cannot / don't want to do, I can assertively acknowledge his need, without ignoring mine. For example, I can recognize and tell him that I understand how important this is to him, but that in that specific situation I cannot help him, listing the reasons, perhaps explaining to him that on another occasion I will not fail him.

- Use phrases of support, openness and encouragement to collaboration. Use phrases that open up a confrontation and dialogue, such as "What do you think? How do you feel? Can you explain better this thing that is not clear to me?"

- Use cooperative phrases that include "we" such as "let's do it, let's see, if we try to ..."

- Formulate sentences that stick to the concrete situation, facts and events ("We had decided something different") and not of presumed intentions ("You do it on purpose to make me angry").

- Make criticisms directed only at behaviors ("You did not help me in this situation") and not at people ("You are selfish").

- Make criticisms only with respect to specific behaviors that occurred at specific times ("You forgot to book dinner at the restaurant") and not generalized ("You always forget everything I ask you to do! You never listen to me!").

www.ingramcontent.com/pod-product-compliance
Lightning Source LLC
Chambersburg PA
CBHW072059110526
44590CB00018B/3241